One Day at a Time

Justyn Rees Larcombe's inspirational story of recovery from overpowering addiction is a wonderful testimony to being lifted out of the deepest pit by the power of Jesus Christ.

Nicky Gumbel

My son's life seemed to be going wonderfully well; I never suspected a secret addiction was destroying everything – until it did! At the time his latest book would have helped us so much, but of course he had to "live it" before he could write it. I know it will be a great resource to us here at Beauty from Ashes, helping to mend lives which have been broken for many different reasons.

Jennifer Rees Larcombe, author, speaker and founder of Beauty from Ashes

This book is a wonderful companion to have, for those of us wishing to understand and grow, finding freedom from addictive behaviours and habits. Justyn speaks with conviction and wisdom about his journey of faith whilst overcoming addiction and finding recovery. His strength about this topic comes from both his personal experiences and the pain that comes hand in hand with destructive habits. Justyn tells his powerful story with great warmth and compassion, which will strike a cord deep in the hearts of those wishing to grow spiritually, whilst tapping into an inner freedom that only God can give.

Emma Heath, Recovery Course Leader, Bournemouth

Also by Justyn Rees Larcombe:

Tails I Lose

ONE DAY AT A TIME

JUSTYN REES LARCOMBE

For Bill

God Bless you

MONARCH
BOOKS

Oxford, UK, and Grand Rapids, USA

Published by Monarch Books
an imprint of
Lion Hudson plc
Wilkinson House, Jordan Hill Road,
Oxford OX2 8DR, England
Email: monarch@lionhudson.com
www.lionhudson.com/monarch

ISBN 978 0 85721 718 9
e-ISBN 978 0 85721 719 6

First edition 2016

Acknowledgments
Unless otherwise marked, scripture quotations are taken from the *Holy Bible, New Living Translation*, copyright © 1996, 2004, 2007 by Tyndale House Foundation. Used by permission of Tyndale House Publishers, Inc., Carol Stream, Illinois 60188. All rights reserved.
Scripture quotations marked "NIV" taken from the Holy Bible, New International Version Anglicised. Copyright © 1979, 1984, 2011 Biblica, formerly International Bible Society. Used by permission of Hodder & Stoughton Ltd, an Hachette UK company. All rights reserved. "NIV" is a registered trademark of Biblica. UK trademark number 1448790.
Scripture quotations marked "ESV" are from The Holy Bible, English Standard Version® (ESV®) copyright © 2001 by Crossway, a publishing ministry of Good News Publishers. All rights reserved.
pp. 101, 201: Extracts from *Breathing Underwater* by Richard Rohr, copyright © Richard Rohr, 2011. Used by permission of St Anthony Messenger Press.

A catalogue record for this book is available from the British Library

Printed and bound in the UK, May 2016, LH26

Dedication

To the real JRL.
For everything, but especially for being there at the lowest time and for
encouraging me to follow in your footsteps.

Contents

Acknowledgments

My thanks must go to the whole Monarch Books team at Lion Hudson. For the faith of Tony Collins; for Rhoda Hardie and the whole PR team, who never seem to stop; but most of all for my Editor, Alison Hull – my perfect foil and one of the wisest people I know. I also want to acknowledge the work of Nigel Skelsey, author of The Recovery Course, and an inspiration to so many of us in Christian recovery. Finally, a big thank you to Chris Mungeam, who is so much more than my agent, mentor, and the person who first told me to write down my story; he's my friend.

Foreword

It's OK to hurt. In the words of the rock band REM's most iconic song, "Everybody hurts".

Most of us won't reach adulthood without some pain, fear, or anxiety. The storms of life hit hard and without warning, and they affect us all: young, old, rich, and poor. Bereavements, disappointments, unfulfilled ambitions, broken relationships, let-downs, ill-health, redundancy, trials, setbacks, and temptations; even success can cause upheaval. And if we don't deal with it, but bury it instead, it is still there.

We find a way of coping with pain because pain is, well, painful. Often our coping strategies are not healthy and their indulgence has consequences that just add more pain on top. For Christians, we fear people finding out about our coping strategies, so we hide them. They become our secret habits. Covering them up causes more complications and can damage our relationships. And even more pain is added on top, so we protect ourselves with our habits, our medication. It's a cycle, but one which can be broken. There is another way – to freedom, fulfilment, and joy, despite life's storms. There is hope.

This book is written for anyone who has a secret habit. For anyone who has lost control and can't stop. Anyone whose life contains a thorn that harms their relationship with their Creator, their family and friends, their work colleagues, or themselves.

This book is for anyone who wants to understand why they keep going back to the same place, even when they don't want to. It's for anyone who wants to break the chains that hold them back from living a free, joyful, and fulfilled life. It's for anyone who wants to take their relationship with God to new heights, but instead of climbing the mountain they just keep walking along the same plateau.

This book is for those of you who have experienced the pain of helplessly watching a loved one struggle with behaviour patterns that harm them and hurt you.

It's for anyone searching for hope in a modern world where it's easier than ever to become ensnared in habits that hold us back from living a life of freedom and joy, free from depression and anxiety.

I wrote this book for those who want to experience the freedom our God has for us in abundance, now and forevermore. And because I want you to know that God loves you completely, unconditionally, and more deeply than you or I will ever understand in this life.

This book is not for those who are perfect already. You can pass.

About the Book

One Day at a Time is not just a memoir. Neither is it just a recovery manual. It's both, and it can be read in different ways. I wanted to write something that can be picked up and enjoyed. Not in a fluffy way, but in a gritty and challenging but wholly satisfying way. It is also intended to be used to help break behaviour patterns, by stating the truth that we are loved by God, unconditionally, and by suggesting simple, practical exercises to enhance that understanding.

If I am honest, I don't really enjoy reading books where the author keeps challenging me to stop reading and do some task or other. You can read this book from cover to cover like a novel if you want to. But I am assuming you want to be free from your habit. So if you want that freedom, you have to do something in response to the words. The exercises at the end of each chapter are there for your benefit. My prayer is that you will be challenged by what I say enough to take the time to take action. You can't read yourself to recovery. You need to take the steps, sequentially, to claim it.

So if you just want to take this book with you and read it like a story, feel free. You may well grasp the truth if you simply do that. If you really need it to transform your life, you may need to follow up on the suggestions I make at the end of each chapter. It's up to you. How much do you want your freedom; how much do you need it in your life?

I am not a psychologist. I haven't studied addiction – at least, not in an academic way. Nor do I pretend to be a qualified counsellor or cognitive therapist. I am just somebody who let an addiction take over my life and have since experienced wonderful freedom from it, through Christ. I want to share my own experiences: nothing more.

Throughout this book, I also share stories of others to enhance the narrative. Where appropriate, their names have been changed to protect their privacy.

The truth

In the 1999 science fiction film, *The Matrix*, the main character, Neo (played by Keanu Reeves), is offered two pills by a character called Morpheus (played by Laurence Fishburne). The red pill and its opposite, the blue pill, represent the choice between embracing the sometimes painful truth of reality (red pill) and the blissful ignorance of illusion (blue pill).

The blue pill would allow Neo to remain in the fabricated reality of the Matrix, therefore living the "ignorance of illusion", while the red pill would lead to his escape from the Matrix and into the real world, therefore living the "truth of reality" even though it is a harsher, more difficult life. Morpheus tells Neo that the Matrix is an illusory world created to prevent humans from discovering that they are slaves to an external influence. He offers Neo both pills – the choice is his.

If you really want to know the truth, take the red pill of an open mind. It may be tougher than continuing to live in an illusory world, the place you have been escaping to. Pray before you read. The words in this book are just words unless the Lord speaks through them to your heart.

Go ahead, take the red pill, and every time you turn a page, keep an open mind. Then and only then can you really say, "And you will know the truth, and the truth will set you free" (John 8:32).

February 2016, Tonbridge

PART 1

FUNDAMENTALS

(STEPS 1 AND 2)

CHAPTER 1

The Journey

"For I know the plans I have for you," says the Lord. "They are plans for good and not for disaster, to give you a future and a hope. In those days when you pray, I will listen. If you look for me wholeheartedly, you will find me. I will be found by you," says the Lord. "I will end your captivity and restore your fortunes. I will gather you out of the nations where I sent you and will bring you home again to your own land."

Jeremiah 29:11–14

I woke early on 7 September 2014, one of the most significant days of my life. I threw back the curtains and let the sunshine flood the room. Outside, the branches of the trees were still, and a light mist hovered above the fields and fragrant orchards. It was early, but the golden sun had already risen above the distant North Downs; I could feel its warmth on my face. I watched for a minute as the morning haze evaporated, bringing the countryside into sharp focus. And my heart beat faster.

Perfect conditions. No turning back now.

Hardly a week had passed over the last two years when I hadn't thought about or prepared, in some way, for today. For more than thirty years I had dreamed of this day. My mobile buzzed. I already knew who the text message was from and had a good idea of the content, but when I read it, my pulse quickened again. To calm myself, I gulped down the cool morning air, knowing I would need every ounce of strength before the day ended.

It's on. Meet @ the marina 9.30.

Stuart, my pilot, was a man of few words. He knew the tides, the currents, and the coastline on both sides of the Pas-de-Calais/Dover Strait; he'd been fishing these waters and guiding swimmers across for twenty-seven years. That short message told me everything I needed to know. We had a window in the weather that should give me enough time to make a solo attempt to swim across the English Channel from England to France. It was really happening.

I felt the adrenaline pumping through my veins as I drove along the M20 towards the rising sun. I found a CD that matched my mood and turned the volume up. Matt Redman was booming out words about needing God. I knew how he felt. I suddenly realized I was gripping the steering wheel so tightly my knuckles were white. I opened the window for more fresh air.

Swimming solo from England to France is considered the most arduous endurance swim in the world. At 33 km as the crow flies, it's not the longest, although no one ever swims in a straight line – the strong tides see to that. It's the cold temperatures (wetsuits are forbidden), the currents, and the busy maritime traffic that make it so tough. The route crosses two of the busiest shipping lanes in the world. By 2015, 4,100 people had climbed Everest; only 1,340 had successfully completed a solo crossing of the Channel. Many more people have won Olympic Gold medals.

At the point where the North Downs meet the sea between the coastal ports of Dover and Folkestone, the road descends steeply, often affording a tantalizing glimpse of France. Sometimes the air is so clear, the French coastline seems close enough to touch, but today it was lost in the haze. France might as well have been a thousand miles away. But the sea looked calm. I knew the sea around Dover harbour well, having swum here most weekends between May and September for the last two years, often swimming for seven or even eight hours on Saturday and then repeating it again on Sunday; it was the closest way to simulate a Channel crossing. The thought of all those endless hours of training reassured me now. I really didn't want to fail and have to give up any more precious weekends. The sea temperature was dropping, the days were getting shorter, and today would be the only opportunity for an attempt this year.

As I drove into the marina car park I noticed what I assumed to be a homeless person slumped against a wall. He was in need of a shave; he looked run down and sunburnt. There were several people around him and I thought no more of it as I parked up and began to get my kit out of the boot of the car. I had packed all I needed for the crossing into a big plastic box the previous evening. Then, in the morning, I had unpacked everything and carefully repacked it all – just as I had done with my equipment before a military operation as an officer in the British Army.

In my kit box were two large flasks of hot water, ready to mix with a high-carbohydrate powder and concentrated fruit cordial. There were two tins of peaches (the salt water causes the throat to swell up and peaches might be the only solid food I could swallow) and a set of small flashing lights: green for the back of my head and orange for my waist. These lights were essential and allowed my safety team to keep sight of me in the dark. I hadn't even trained to swim with my support boat in the daylight, let alone the dark. I hoped I would make it across before night fell and the temperature dropped. I would worry about that if and when it happened.

The liquid would be thrown to me at regular intervals in a plastic carton, tied to the support boat by a cord. I would have to take on the fluid while in the water because if I were even to touch the boat I would be disqualified by the observer. He would be there to ratify the swim and keep an eye on my condition, looking out for signs of hypothermia and exhaustion. Last year and the year before there had been fatalities. Both swimmers, in sight of the French coast, had tried to battle through extreme fatigue. It was small consolation to know that defibrillators were now mandatory equipment on all the support boats.

"Hey, Mr Serious, how you feeling?"

I smiled as I was greeted by Carolyn, an open water swimmer I had trained with over the summer. She had kindly volunteered to give up a day and probably most of the night to feed me and offer encouragement. Although not yet a Channel swimmer herself, she was hugely experienced and had acted as an observer on several occasions. I knew her experience, reassurance, encouragement, and cheerful humour would be invaluable to me. I also knew if she told me to get out of the water during the crossing, it would be for a good reason. I trusted her completely.

"I feel fine. Bit nervous, I guess, but better than that poor chap looks," I said, nodding towards the man who I had assumed slept out on the streets. He was still slumped against the wall.

"He's just missed beating the record for the longest crossing. He was in the water for more than twenty-seven hours."

I looked over with a new mix of admiration and horror. I was certain I didn't have the same stamina. The thought of getting back in my car and driving off was very appealing at that precise moment.

"Come on then, podge," said Carolyn, with one of her most reassuring looks. "Let's go and find the *Sea Leopard*, or we'll miss the tide." I followed her, struggling with the weight of my kit box. I did feel a bit of a podge as I waddled down the ramp towards the dock where my pilot and the observer were busily preparing the boat for departure. I had taken the advice to "carb-load" very seriously!

An hour later I knew it was on for sure. I had been this far before, turning up at the marina at 10 p.m. just three weeks ago. But the attempt had been aborted, owing to high winds. Physically, I had been at my peak back then, having tapered off my long swims for a week before and made sure I took on extra calories. I had been told I would lose at least a stone in body weight as my body consumed the available energy and then ate into my fat reserves and finally into muscle – which would be quite painful. When that attempt was aborted, I had made myself available at six hours' notice. It had meant I couldn't really train, in case I received the call to go. I wanted enough fat reserves to avoid the pain, so I forced myself to eat five meals a day. Three weeks on a forced diet with no long training swims meant I had lost some of my conditioning!

I looked out at a flat sea as the converted fishing boat, *Sea Leopard*, chugged out of the protection of the marina towards Shakespeare Beach – the traditional start point midway between Folkestone and Dover.

I didn't feel much like talking, so I was grateful to Carolyn for keeping up a cheerful banter as I began my final preparations. A common misconception is the belief that copious amounts of goose fat will provide insulation. I made sure I applied Vaseline where parts of my body would rub to prevent chafing, and I hoped that the Vaseline would offer some protection against the stinging tentacles of the jellyfish I expected to swim through.

"OK, Justyn, almost time now. I need to run through the safety brief with you, explain my role, and one or two rules you need to be aware of." My observer, Phil, was an ex-military policeman whose presence in the boat, like Caroline's, was hugely reassuring.

The safety briefing felt very formal and I admit now, looking back, that I was scared. I was scared of the unknown. Would my shoulders give up halfway? What if the wind picked up and it got dark? Would I manage twelve hours of drinking high-energy drinks without some reaction from my stomach? What about the huge container ships I would probably encounter, like *The Seawise Giant*, at 458 metres long, 69 metres wide, and 350 metres high? Would they see me in time to stop?

As I looked out across the stretch of water I had dreamed of swimming, I felt a real sense of the presence of God. It felt right somehow that I was here today. Not because it would raise money for charity, or make me feel good about myself. It was more that this was a significant moment, an event that had been predestined. I had a sense of being at one with his will for my life, doing the right thing, at the right time, in the right place. So I prayed: "I'm not strong enough to do this on my own. Help me, Lord."

And then I felt peace. Complete and total calm, like the calm sea I was looking at. I couldn't do anything about the weather; I couldn't see the coast of France; I had to trust Stuart, my pilot, to navigate and get me there safely. I accepted that there might be challenges beyond my control. All I could do was manage the things I had any control over. I had trained hard and, although I wasn't at my peak, I could do nothing more than give it my all.

Stuart cut the engine, and before I dived in and swam to the beach that was to be my start point, he said something to me I will never forget: "See it like a journey. Don't try and tackle it all at once. Take it steady and just make sure you follow each stroke by another one. You keep doing that and you'll reach your destination. Stay close to the boat."

Minutes later I was standing on the beach, looking out across the sea. I couldn't see where I was going; I had no idea what route I would take or how long I would be in the water. But I trusted the team to get me there safely, to navigate through the shipping and the tides and to keep me fed. All I had to do was take one stroke after another. And then the hooter sounded, I dived into the cool, flat water. My journey had begun.

Reflections

Just twenty-two months before, I thought I had reached the end of the road. After three crazy years I had lost everything because of my addiction to online gambling, including my home, my job and three-quarters of a million pounds. My wife had left me and taken our young boys with her. She was right to leave. My life had been in a free fall of self-destruction and, heavily in debt, I had been totally hooked on gambling. The only way out I could see was to take my life.

But that wasn't the end. Instead of taking my own life, I gave it back to the God I had known for much of my life. I had pushed him away through arrogance and pride when I found financial success in business. And so I discovered the end was just the beginning. The God of grace heard me when I cried out to him in desperation, and he restored my life in a very short time. Emma, my wife, had recently moved back in with me and we were a family once more in a new home, debt free, and with my priorities in the right order.

But how easy it had been to let what had started as just a small secret habit turn into something destructive, in such a short time. If we are honest with ourselves, we all have secret habits: eating, watching pornography, drinking, maybe spending too much money. They might not be as destructive as I allowed mine to become, but if left unchecked, they will cause damage to our relationships with Christ, with our loved ones, and with ourselves. Before God there are no secrets. He knows our hearts.

Life is a journey. None of us is perfect, but if we are to reach the destination God has for each of us and to live in the here and now, we need to follow where Christ leads us. We must accept the truth that he loves us abundantly, and nothing we can ever do will make him love us more or love us any less. There may be suffering on our journey, and we will make mistakes, but I would like to share my experience of how we can avoid the distractions of those secret habits that look so tempting, so harmless, and so trivial – but are so totally wrong.

We all have our own journeys to follow, and Christ has a path for each of us. Come and share my journey for a while, and see how my search for truth in the world around me culminated in the staggering and completely transformational realization that the truth of God's love was inside me all along.

I took my first stroke and followed it with another. I knew my strokes weren't perfect. They could have been more efficient, more powerful, but I also knew all I had to do was keep turning my arms. At times, I thought about giving up and going back to the safety of the harbour. I also longed to arrive at my destination, to feel dry land under my feet. But I knew I had to live in the moment, to concentrate all my energy and all my thoughts in the present. In my mind I knew I just had to keep taking another stroke. I tried not to think of the end and instead I concentrated on each hour, on making it to the next feed time.

If you are in the midst of an addiction and you can't see the end, don't even try. Just get through the next hour, then the next day. Don't try and tackle the whole thing at once. Just don't have the next drink or place the next bet.

The hardest thing about recovery is that it is painful at first, because what you are seeking to do is to take away your medicine, to take away the crutch you have been leaning on. Without medication, you have to face up to the issues that made you use in the first place. You feel the pain, but rather than running from it, you have to deal with it. That means, at first, you have to walk with a limp. We have to make ourselves vulnerable, to get rid of the pride, and accept that we are flawed, either through circumstances or by our own actions.

When we do that, it is a transformational moment because, as Christians, when we make ourselves vulnerable we realize how totally loved we are by God. I found that when I made myself vulnerable, when I made the decision not to run to my medication of choice, God met me there and he healed me. He mended the long-term issues I was carrying, had been carrying for almost all my life.

I knew I wouldn't get to France with one mighty pull. It would take time. I had also come to realize I would never reach the perfect destination my Creator had for me in one go. When I realized my recovery and my whole life was a journey, it made things easier to grasp. Living life in the here and now was what mattered; one day at a time.

If it helps you, picture yourself in the car of your choice. You can start your engine if you like, but don't set off just yet. There are a few things you need to know before you start. The first is to establish your "start line".

Review

Recovery is a journey. Take it one day at a time and don't be discouraged if you fall. You can't reach your destination instantly, so be patient. This is a test of endurance, not a sprint.

Exercise

Take a moment to be grateful for the present. Go for a walk if you have time, and let go of the past, all your successes and failures. Just for a moment, don't worry about the future. During your time out, accept that it may take time to overcome your secret habits.

CHAPTER 2

The Start Line

"For I am about to do something new.
See I have already begun! Do you not see it?
I will make a pathway through the wilderness.
I will create rivers in the dry wasteland."

Isaiah 43:19

I love to visit a place in the south west corner of the largest of the Channel Islands, Jersey. The stunning cliffs on both sides protect a long, sandy, south-facing beach. When I walk on that beach, or swim across the bay, I feel alive. The sea is clear blue almost all year round. I enjoy walking barefoot along the water's edge, feeling the power of the waves as they roll up and then retreat again, on the flat golden sand. I like to watch the sun rise; the warm light, even in winter, transforms the water to a sea of liquid gold. It's one of my "thin" places, where I feel the presence of the Creator God, my Abba.

One perfect spring morning, as I walked across the sand, I made a promise that I would turn my back on my habit forever. I hadn't gambled for more than a year, but I wanted to make a vow, a covenant, and I wanted some sign or symbol of my promise. I looked around for a beautiful shell or something significant that just happened to be washed up on the beach that morning, something I could look at if I felt tempted, that would remind me of my promise. But I found nothing more than driftwood and worm casts in the sand. I began to feel despondent. Perhaps it was a mistake to make such a promise? I knew how weak and frail I was, how many wrong turns I'd made in my life. Who was I kidding that my flawed promises would mean anything to such an immense, powerful God?

I almost missed it as I trudged back towards the car park. It was a very plain and ordinary grey stone, quite small and insignificant. At first it looked like every other stone I had rejected as too common to mean anything. But something made me pick the stone up.

I turned it over, and there on the back of the stone was a perfect straight line. The creamy white colour of the single line stood out against the plain dark grey background. But as I held it, the stone dried and the clarity of the line faded in the sea breeze. I dipped it in a nearby pool and the line returned, as clear as before.

For me, that line represented the promise I had made. It was my "start line". On one side of the line lay my past: all the pain, the hurt, the destruction, the lies, the broken and damaged relationships, the time I had misspent gambling on my computer when I should have been playing with my children and making them laugh, and feel secure and loved. There too were all the opportunities I had missed to make my beautiful wife smile, and to provide the intimacy she had longed for. I had been too depressed or elated to recognize the signs and had simply rolled over and fallen asleep without even kissing her goodnight. On that same side of the line were my regrets, the money I had squandered, the financial security I had wrecked, the guilt I felt, the humiliation, and the shame. There was the pride that for so long had stopped me from getting the help I needed.

On the other side of the line, the larger part of the stone, lay hope, reconciliation, a bright future, the joy of freedom, and another chance to live a full and satisfying life. On that side of the line was a new set of priorities where people, not things, are the most important. On that side of the line was salvation.

As I listened to the sound of the crashing waves, the gulls calling as they circled above, and felt the touch of cool, salty wind on my face, I realized that unless I remained covered by the eternal, living water of Christ, that line would disappear. Everything I had left behind would return to swallow me up again. I had no right to make any promises to God. All I could do was ask for his grace, for a greater sense of the depth of his love for me. Without his touch on the stone of my life, there could be no permanent line.

I still have the stone. I look at it from time to time. When it's dry, you can't see the line. Only when it's wet does it really remind me of the incredible gift of freedom I was given, on the day he touched my heart.

If you have decided to turn your back on something that's been pulling you down, before you do anything else, find your own start line. It may be a boundary fence or a gate, or just a line you draw on paper. It could be a place you create in your mind, or a real place. Something tangible is good if you are anything like me, and something linear!

The start line is important because it represents the choice you make to leave your habit and all the bad stuff that goes with it behind you. It represents a choice only you can make. There is hope; there is help; there is healing. Your freedom is a gift that awaits you. But you have to choose to accept the gift, to unwrap it. It was there for me long before I chose to ask for help. To move forward from my start line, the only thing I needed to do was reach out for it, to decide to choose freedom and escape my cycle of addiction. It's the thing that only you can do, that you have to do on your own. No one can choose for you to recover – except you.

The line might move a few times before it becomes permanent, but remember, it can only exist with the help of Christ; so ask him to help you draw it. He is asking you to make a decision, and you have to choose which side of the line you want to stand on. He can help you draw the line, but he leaves the decision to you.

You will need that line for the exercise at the end of this chapter. It's a line you will come to know well because you will need to go back there and keep dumping negative things on the other side. You don't want to leave anything negative on your side, anything that will drag you back. Regret was a hard one for me. It meant I kept looking backwards and couldn't see where I was heading.

Once you have your start line, you can be reflective. In the next chapter we can leave our start line and, while we are on our journey forward, we can try to answer the question, "Why am I here?"

Review

Your start line is the beginning of your journey. On one side are all the destructive, negative things associated with your habit. On the other is freedom.

Exercise

On a large blank page, draw a line down the middle. On one side of the line, write everything negative you can think of that relates to your habit: how it makes you feel, the effect it has on others, etc.

Now, on the other side of the line, write down what your freedom looks like and all the good things that will happen when you leave your habit behind your start line.

CHAPTER 3

Getting to Know You

*For I do not understand my own actions. For I do not do what I want,
but I do the very thing I hate. Now if I do what I do not want, I
agree with the law, that it is good. So now it is no longer I who do it,
but sin that dwells within me. For I know that nothing good dwells in
me, that is, in my flesh. For I have the desire to do what is right, but
not the ability to carry it out. For I do not do the good I want, but the
evil I do not want is what I keep on doing.*

Romans 7:15–19 (ESV UK)

Why?

It was early January, one of those clear, crisp, winter days when
everything feels new. The bright sun was low in an electric blue
sky, above the white frosted fields and frozen puddles. I glanced
at my watch. It was time to turn back. I had been walking in the
beautiful countryside near my mother's home for two hours.
Without a full-time job, there was little else to occupy my time back
then. To counter the cold I wore a fleece coat and woollen scarf.
The scarf had been a present from Emma on my fortieth birthday,
almost three years before; before everything, in a different lifetime.
The scarf still had a faint smell that reminded me of my home,
my two young boys, and being part of a family. But each day the
smell became fainter, and soon this little link to my past would be
lost. Another family now lived in the house I had called home. I
was thinking. I had plenty of time to reflect now my mind wasn't

occupied by the crazy thoughts of a twenty-four-hour compulsive gambler.

I followed the frozen path as it led me out of a thick chestnut wood to a recently cleared area. Fresh sawdust decorated the mud around the tree stumps. After the darkness of the forest, I stood in the winter sunshine, blinking at the view of the Kent and Sussex countryside. I could see for miles.

Quite suddenly, I heard a voice. It was familiar because the voice was my own. "How on earth did that just happen?"

It was barely six weeks after my crash, and the shock of that horrible day was, at last, beginning to fade. On that day, my world had finally come tumbling down around me. It had been a day of humiliation, the worst day of my life. But it had also been the first day of a new and infinitely better life, when I had been cut back to a tree stump, like those I was now surrounded by. It had started with me still pretending to be a successful businessman, even though I had lost my job months before, and ended with me on my knees, broken, asking God to forgive me, to fix me. I was calling on the God I had once known intimately and then turned my back on, for three destructive years. I was penniless, separated from my wife and children, without a job, and with only a black bin liner of old clothes and some pictures to call my own. I had lost my home and discovered I was £73,000 in debt.

I wanted to understand why I could have had such a spectacular fall. Why, in the space of three years, had I gone from being a successful businessman at the top of my game, a loving husband, a new father, a financially secure home owner with a bright future ahead of me – to a homeless, lonely gambling addict? Now, as I asked myself "Why?", I realized I didn't know myself – and I never had truly known myself at any point in my past.

I knew *how to behave*: how to be a good employee, a good husband, a good father, a good son, even a good Christian. And where I wasn't much good, I became a good actor; I pretended. What I lacked in ability I made up for in bravado, in pretence. But I didn't really know what was driving me. Most importantly, I didn't know the pain I carried inside. I didn't acknowledge it. It became a ticking time bomb. Had I known how much pain I had packed away inside, maybe my crash would never have happened. What would have happened if I had known the truth that I was unconditionally loved? Or realized that a fear of abandonment from an incident in my childhood would cause me, for the next thirty years of my life, to base my self-worth on others' perceptions of me, driving me relentlessly into a frenzy of unquenchable achievement and outward success?

I learnt from a very early age the importance of being independent, that showing emotions was something men just didn't do. I lost the innocence of childhood and learnt to be independent, not to trust anyone except myself, because I never knew when they would leave. And when my father did leave us all to make a new home, I shrugged it off and pretended it didn't matter. By then I was serving in the army, in an environment where any sign of emotion was seen as weakness. So I bottled it all up and put a big cork in the top.

In the same bottle went my disappointment when I was rejected as a military pilot. I had no time to deal with that rejection because I was immediately posted to another regiment which was about to deploy on an operational tour.

The bottle was filling up when I got back from Bosnia, a country I witnessed horrifically tearing itself apart, to discover my first wife had been having an affair. Still in shock from witnessing at first hand the aftermath of ethnic cleansing on a huge scale, I cursed myself for being stupid enough to trust anyone but myself. My issues with abandonment were reaffirmed. But I refused to admit I felt any pain and convinced myself everything was fine because I could still see my young son, Harry, regularly. Later, having remarried, I lost that regular access to the happy, fun-filled weekends, when my ex-wife took Harry to live with her and her new husband in the Channel Islands. That blow coincided with the discovery that the baby I had with my new wife had suffered a stroke at birth and the damage to his brain would cause permanent disablement.

When we almost lost him during a serious and prolonged epileptic fit just before his first birthday, something had to give; the cork was under huge pressure. I had no idea how to manage my emotions or how to talk about my feelings. When my false bubble of success and achievement finally burst, I either had to find help and admit I couldn't cope – or find another coping strategy. Like a fool, I chose the second option, though I wasn't consciously doing so. And my world came crashing down.

I have a photograph I sometimes look at to remind me of that time. It was taken by Emma, the girl of my dreams, just after we were married. I met her at a time when I was battered and bruised by the failure of my first marriage. I had no intention of making another mistake in relationships and had decided to live a happy life on my own. I felt that was my calling and had come to terms with it. Then I met Emma and fell in love. I never believed in love at first sight until that day.

Emma took the photo on the Isle of Capri while I reclined in an infinity pool. Just behind my rather smug face, in the distance across the Bay of Naples and simmering in a heat haze, is Mount Vesuvius. Still an active volcano, it is famous for the sudden and devastating eruption that led to the destruction of the prosperous Roman city of Pompeii in AD 79. On the outside, at this point my life probably looked quite good. I worked in the City of London and earned a good wage, we owned our own home, we drove lovely cars and enjoyed luxurious holidays. Matty had been born but not yet diagnosed with his disability. I should have been happy. But inside me, the cork was about to come flying off. My very own Mount Vesuvius was about to erupt.

I discovered gambling by chance, just a couple of weeks after Matty's first fit. I saw an advertisement on TV. It looked fun. When I realized placing money on an outcome, however unlikely, could alter my feelings, I was wired in very quickly. Gambling gave me an escape from pain I hadn't even acknowledged existed, and provided me with an opportunity to succeed. It also gave me access to the adrenaline I craved and had lived off for most of my life. This adrenaline was in short supply at this point, for a man who felt that he had made it in life. The greater the risk, the more adrenaline flowed. But, like alcohol, the body becomes accustomed to the drug and my stakes had to increase to generate the same buzz.

When I realized I was losing more than winning, my stakes increased as I tried to cover my losses. Gambling my money, then borrowed money, and then money that belonged to my wife gave me the high I felt when I jumped out of aeroplanes in the army. I gradually became dependent on it. For a time, while I was winning, I felt better. Gambling provided a place for me to hide from a reality that was becoming increasingly stressful, caused by my own stupidity. The result was a spiral of destruction and, within three years, complete carnage.

I was a Christian, but a successful career in the City of London had led me to become full of pride in my own achievements. I had stopped going to church and reading my Bible each day. In fact, the only time I prayed in the year before I placed my first bet was to cry out to God to save Matty after he stopped breathing during his first epileptic fit. The Lord answered that prayer in the form of our next door neighbour, a retired surgeon. He was returning from a shopping trip when he found me giving mouth-to-mouth resuscitation to my son in the back of my car. But still I didn't turn back to God or ask him to help carry my pain. I don't think I even thanked him when Matty recovered. I stopped living in the light; I stopped reading the Bible. My defences were down.

I'm not saying that pain will always lead to destructive behaviour. But it needs to be dealt with. Neither is it an excuse for our actions. I take full responsibility for the course my life took. I also gladly accept God's grace for forgiving and restoring me. Blaming our addictive or secretive behaviour on anyone or anything without taking full responsibility is a form of denial. Denial is the single biggest obstacle that prevents any recovery, and it will lead to relapse if it is allowed back over your start line at any stage during the recovery process – and the recovery process lasts as long as our lives do.

The importance of knowing

Understanding ourselves and accepting the existence of pain, even if we don't know where it comes from, means we can begin to deal with it more effectively. For those who have the painful and difficult experience of watching helplessly as a loved one reaches for their destructive "medication" of choice, this understanding helps increase empathy and initiate forgiveness. But for forgiveness to come, it needs a willingness to change on the part of the addict.

Addicts don't become addicts by choice. You can imagine the classroom discussion on a child's first day at school. The teacher gathers all the children round in a circle and one by one she asks them what they want to be when they grow up. They might say a fireman, a nurse, a doctor, or whatever their own parent's profession may be, but no one says, "I want to be a heroin addict," or "I want to be an alcoholic."

I plead with those who have to watch loved ones self-destruct, to understand that we use our habits and compulsions to medicate the pain that we all carry with us into adulthood. If we grasp that fact then we can begin to understand the psyche of the addict. In his book *Abba's Child*, Brennan Manning, himself a recovering alcoholic, wonderfully captures the importance of understanding the pain that that sits behind compulsive behaviour. He says that understanding triggers the compassion that hastens forgiveness. This is the secret that allows us to forgive anyone anything, and in doing so we discover it sets us free. Forgiveness sets us free in the perfect realization that, in our resentment against others, we were the captive. The ability to find forgiveness for our enemy matures when we discover where our enemy cries. That's not to say the addict who takes no responsibility to change has a right to demand infinite forgiveness from those they hurt each day.

My son Matty is now a huge 7-year-old. As well as epilepsy and right-side hemiplegia, a form of cerebral palsy caused by the stroke he suffered at birth, he is autistic. In crowded or noisy places he can suffer from sensory overload, which manifests itself when he lashes out or pushes anyone who stands in his way. This is so hard to manage. When he pushes an adult, it's not so bad: we just apologize. But when he pushes over a smaller child, it can lead to conflict from a quite rightly protective parent. It's not so easy to explain, while I am being throttled by an angry father, that my son, who looks normal in every way, didn't push over the screaming young girl on purpose. But when they hear the explanation, they usually smile kindly. They *understand* his behaviour. Usually!

As I stood in the clearing on that beautiful winter's day, with my life stripped back down to a stump, I didn't receive any answers to my question, "How did that happen?" The revelation that I had spent my life in fear of abandonment, searching for reassurance in the approval of others while bottling up pain, resentment, fear, hurt, unfulfilled ambition, and disappointment came to me a few months later. It was when I started writing my first book, *Tails I Lose*.[1]

I wanted to share my story, to let people know there is a downside to gambling. We are bombarded by a deluge of gambling advertising twenty-four hours a day on the TV, in the papers, on social media – it feels like almost everywhere – that says, "Gambling is an entertaining, social, fun, and financially rewarding activity." I wanted people to know that, for me and for hundreds of thousands of others, our experiences of gambling are quite the opposite.

However, as I started to write, I didn't know there would be other benefits. In fact, it was very painful at first. I thought I was doing something wrong, so I called my editor, Ali. "Something's

---

1   Lion Books, 2014.

not right. Every time I try and write a sentence, I end up crying so much I can't see what I've written," I said.

Ali wasn't fazed, and her reply was brilliant. "It's fine. Good writing is like sitting down at your keyboard and opening up a vein. You need to bleed a bit to take your readers with you. If you don't, your story will feel too removed, like you're a spectator and not actually experiencing it."

It was painful, but I learnt so much in writing out the story of my life. I came to see patterns around things that were happening and had happened in different parts of my life. It helped me to understand myself better and gave me a few extra tools to be able to deal with the pressures and fastballs that life does and will go on throwing at us from time to time.

I had learnt in the army never to open up. No one liked the officers' mess bore who always tries to steer every conversation round to something he has done or achieved, giving his opinion on everything as though it is the definitive precedent. In order to be popular, I learnt not to talk about myself, my feelings or my achievements. I discovered that it was better for my popularity to ask others about theirs. The problem with this, though, is that I also lost the art of being able to express my feelings and emotions. I ended up trying to please others all the time, in order to achieve popularity. If I ever ventured my own opinion, it was always based on what I thought those listening would want to hear. I also believed I was the only one who could solve all the problems I faced. Asking for help, as I have said, would have been an impossible admission of failure.

Through writing my story down, I now understand that I have a nature which is "full on". Many people call it an addictive personality. I also accept that I am hugely competitive by nature. I hate to lose and I am a huge optimist. So my glass is either completely full or completely empty. I'm either "in" 100 per cent or not in at all.

Recognize those traits? Through my work, I have the privilege of working with professional sportspeople around the issue of gambling. The need for adrenaline and the desire to win are traits I share with many of those I work with. I just wish I shared their talents!

When it comes to habits, this means I have to be very, very careful. I have to be accountable, open, and honest. When I do something I need to make sure I do it openly. If we are not honest enough to be ourselves in every situation, it will lead to conflict and cause stress. Stress and conflict lead to trouble for those with a full-on personality. If we manage to be honest in every situation – secretly, privately, and publicly – we defeat conflict, we lose the need to medicate, we are set free. But it's only in the incredible realization of the truth that we are loved and accepted for who we are, warts and all, that we are able to be genuine, not fearing what others will think of us, and even beginning to actually quite like ourselves. It is there, standing in the light of this perfect truth, that we find the holy grail of recovery, the truth of God's unconditional and all-encompassing love for us, as we are – not as we would pretend to be.

If I understand that I won't be satisfied with a small helping of food or with one glass of wine, that I will always crave another, I have a really powerful tool to hand that will help me plan ahead and avoid certain activities that might lead me to an unhealthy behaviour pattern. If I understand that my mind lies to me and tells me I need another helping to be happy, I can deal with it. It can also help those around me because they can help me to stay honest, keep me accountable, and avoid inadvertently putting something in front of me that might not be good for me. Simple stuff, but it is very effective.

If I get to know myself well enough to understand that I have a propensity to look for approval in other people to provide my self-worth, I can begin to see my weak attempts to impress others for what they are: a sham that cloaks the real me and represses my spirit.

Getting to know yourself is particularly good for those

struggling with compulsive or repetitive habits, and also for those affected by them. There are some simple ways you can get to know yourself better. Take a look at the exercises section at the end of this chapter. For me, I had to spend time on my own, and particularly on my own listening to my Creator through his word.

As you get to know yourself a bit better, I need to make one last point. It's an issue which some find hard to accept, and it can cause some conflict within the family unit. Don't let it. Just be honest and open. There have been a number of studies that suggest a genetic link can be passed between generations. There may well be an increased chance of us developing addictive behaviours if our parents also had compulsive and destructive habits, either openly or secretively. We can't use this as an excuse to blame others or as a tool to make our parents feel bad. We mustn't do that because, again, it's a way to avoid taking responsibility, a form of denial. But we should be aware of it so we can better understand ourselves. So if you are an addict and you have children, use this as an even greater motivation to clean up your act. You know the misery of addiction. But don't feel guilty. Guilt is one of the things that can perpetuate or even initiate destructive behaviour.

I was speaking to a group of professional rugby players recently. After my talk, one of them asked me if I felt my addiction had been inherited. I had to tell him I wasn't aware of any issues, although I did think it was common. He told me about a discussion he had had with his father when he was just twelve. He said his father told him that his grandfather had been an alcoholic, and his father before him. As I looked up at this huge figure, I realized that his desire not to fall into a destructive habit had probably driven him on to the international success he was now enjoying. It reminded me that a predisposition to become addicted to things can be a strength if understood and used correctly.

Having benefitted from a few months of introspection in writing my autobiography, I accept I have a personality that is more likely to lead to repetitive behaviour if I pursue secret habits at times of emotional upheaval. A combination of my character, the external environment, and my emotional state: they were all equally important and all had a part to play in my downfall. The age-old conundrum is nature versus nurture: are we born a certain way or does the way we are brought up make us turn out that way? It's both. If you can accept that and get to know yourself better, you will be better prepared to prevent or overcome addictive behaviour.

The benefits of knowing

Now for the good part. When we allow Christ to come into our lives – and that means every aspect of our lives – he can deal with the pain and the hurt. He can even gently show you pain you have been storing up, pain that has to be dealt with. There are many comforting verses in the Bible. My favourite verse is also one of the most simple:

> *The Lord is close to the brokenhearted;*
> *he rescues those whose spirits are crushed.*
>
> **Psalm 34:18**

This verse has two aspects. Firstly, the psalmist accepts that we may well suffer pain and a broken heart. We are not promised a life without pain, only that in our pain God will be close to us. Secondly, God can and will rescue us if we allow him. It took me three years, maybe longer, of thinking I could rescue myself from my "crushed spirit". In fact, I just succeeded in crushing myself even more. I actually believed that if I ignored my pain or tried to anesthetize it by my habit, my medicine of choice, it would go away. But it always came back, generally worse than it had been before. It took one simple prayer for God to rescue me. The outward behaviour he altered quickly; my inner healing took longer. Be prepared for the long haul. It's going to take time. Recognize that recovery is neither fast nor simple, but it is so very attainable, if we are open to it. If we want to find freedom, we can and will be rescued!

I also love God's promise to us about pain in the time to come. It's right at the end of the Bible:

> *He will wipe away every tear from their eyes, and there will be no more death or sorrow or crying or pain. All these things are gone forever.*

Revelation 21:4

To get to know yourself, you have to be honest. C. S. Lewis makes a good point that perhaps not all pain is a bad thing in the long run:

> *[Pain] removes the veil; it plants the flag of truth within the fortress of a rebel soul.*[2]

Truth is very important. We need to be truthful to ourselves, and to others, and to know the most important truth of all: that God's love for us is never-ending.

It was this last truth that, for me, was the final piece in the complex jigsaw of my life. I had come to know myself, but most importantly I came to know that I was loved in spite of my faults and weaknesses. That truth set me free: free to be myself, free not to look for or demand the reassurance of others' approval, free not to need approval by succeeding in shallow worldly things like business, sport, or finance. I was free to be the unhappy adolescent who had grown into a frightened, vulnerable, flawed adult, but who was totally loved by God and forgiven by his grace.

That same truth can set you free.

If you have been holding on to pain, thinking you can manage it within the "fortress of [your] rebel soul", then perhaps it's time to let down the drawbridge and let Christ back in. Let him come in and plant the flag of truth in your heart behind your battlements,

---

2   C. S. Lewis, *The Problem of Pain* (1940).

behind the wall you have built. Let him into that place where you are most vulnerable, the inner keep you have spent your life fortifying. Then you can get to know yourself and begin to be really honest. You are on the right side of the start line, but now you need to get out of the car, hand over the keys to your Creator, get comfortable in the passenger seat, and wait for the journey of your life.

If you find that concept scary or difficult, take a trip to chapter seven where we look at control in more detail, then come back. For me, letting go and accepting that I needed help, that I couldn't fix things on my own, was really hard to do. But when I did, it was a transformational moment, a moment when I wondered, "Why didn't I do this before?"

Review

Getting to know yourself is important in recovery. Try to understand your inner motives. This may take time, and you will need to be prepared for some pain. The more in touch you are with your emotions, the easier it will be to identify the patterns of behaviour that cause you to reach for your medication.

Exercise

Answer the following ten questions honestly:

- Do you feel comfortable in your own company, or do you seek to fill time with other people, TV, social media?

- Are you content with the present, do you miss the past, or are you impatient to move on to the next thing?

- Are you aware of a particularly painful event in your life? Have you dealt with the pain, or do you feel it's all in the past and not worth stirring up now?

- When you look in the mirror, what do you feel?

- Do you worry about the future?

- What do you like to do to unwind at the end of a hard day/week?

- In a crisis, do you seek support and help, or prefer to deal with the issue yourself?

- Are you concerned that others are dependent on you and you worry you might let them down?

- Do you take time each evening to think about the day and put right any wrongs you may have caused?

- Do you find it easy to accept responsibility and say you are sorry when you are at fault?

- Write your life story. Take as long as you have time for. Start with your first memory and bring the story right up to date.

- Decide to spend some time alone each day. Take a walk in a park or in the countryside. Leave your music behind!

- Wake a bit earlier each day and dip into the most precious thing you own. Read God's word each day. No excuses.

CHAPTER 4

What is an Addiction?
(Steps 1 and 2)

Step 1: "We admitted we were powerless over our addiction and that our lives had become unmanageable."

Step 2: "We came to believe that a power greater than ourselves could restore us to sanity."

Insanity is doing the same thing over and over again and expecting different results.

Albert Einstein

There are many definitions of addiction. I like the Farlex Medical Dictionary version because it's simple: "Addiction is a persistent, compulsive dependence on a behaviour or substance."

Many researchers and psychiatrists subdivide addiction into two types: substance addictions (for example, alcoholism, drug abuse, and smoking) and process addictions (for example, gambling, spending, shopping, eating, and sexual activity). However, most of them can be linked with the release of adrenaline or other chemicals into the bloodstream. They also make the point that many addicts suffer from more than one addiction, although one behaviour pattern is generally more predominant at any one time.

It's not a problem unless it's a problem

I recently met a man called John who was broken by his addiction to alcohol. He said he had always been a drinker, but it had never been a problem until he got married. He was a journalist, and it was quite normal for him to have lunch in the pub and join his colleagues for a drink after work. In fact, if he hadn't joined them he would have been the odd one out. He thought nothing of drinking a bottle of wine and a few more beers with the takeaway he bought on the walk back from the station each night.

Then John met and fell in love with a beautiful girl called Michelle, and they got married. He continued to drink with his workmates, but this began to become an issue when he got back late and invariably opened his usual bottle of wine, which he drank by himself. Michelle felt left out, they stopped talking, and their time together was strained.

The marriage fell apart and John lost his job when the paper he worked for closed down suddenly. But he didn't stop drinking. Instead, he drank more to escape the pain of loss in his life. He said to me, "I never saw my drinking as a problem until I got married and it became a problem for someone else. By then I couldn't control it."

For me, that is precisely the point when a habit becomes an addiction: when it becomes a problem – whether for you, your family, your work colleagues, or anyone who is affected by your habit in a negative way. Take ownership: if *your* behaviour is a problem for anyone, it's a problem for you. But what often happens is you finally realize that what has seemed so harmless is now a problem, but you can't stop; you have become *dependent* on either the substance or the process. So your first reaction is to deny it and see it as their problem, those people around you, not your problem. Or you try to minimize the impact: you avoid arguments and start covering up. You might hide a bottle or two and drink in secret.

When you do that, you start to isolate yourself and do things in the darkness. When we pull down the blinds, our habits can spiral out of control.

We need to see the bigger picture. Sometimes we drink, or we eat, or we use, or we act, to escape from something. We need to understand that if we do this, instead of dealing with the issue by talking it through and bringing it into the light before God, then it gets worse. We damage ourselves and others. The underlying issue remains there, and the guilt of what we are doing and the pain caused to those around us add to it. The underlying issue gets worse.

We can justify our actions by comparing ourselves with others. We can say we don't really have a problem, compared to someone else, and so we avoid the diagnosis, the label of "addict", and never really address the issue. But then we can't find peace or the freedom to live how Christ wants us to live. The habit we have of escaping blocks our intimacy with God, because we feel guilty afterwards. It harms our relationships with the people we love. It damages the way we see ourselves. All these things create more pain and increase our desire to escape. It's a vicious circle, one the deceiver just loves to watch because he sees us tearing ourselves apart and he hardly has to lift a finger.

I gave a talk just a few days ago, and afterwards an elderly lady came up to me after everyone else had gone. She said a little thank you for my talk and turned to leave, but I sensed her loneliness and that she wanted to say more, so I tried to strike up a conversation. Eventually she told me what I think she had wanted to say. When she was an 11-year-old girl, her dad used to finish work early and come and meet her from school. It was always on a Thursday because that was the day her mother worked late, cleaning at the "big house". It was always the best part of the week for her because her dad worked hard and she rarely spent much time with him. I can picture her as a little schoolgirl, saving up all her news, her small achievements, and the things that matter to an 11-year-old. But one day her dad was late. This would have been in the days before mobile phones, so she did the right thing and waited. Eventually, by the time darkness fell, her dad arrived. She knew he had been to the pub because she could smell it. It wasn't the first time, and it would not be the last.

When they got home, rather than making her a sandwich and chatting, playing cards, or reading together, her dad lay down on the sofa and fell asleep. She couldn't wake him, even though she tried many times. In the end she just went to her bedroom and cried herself to sleep.

This lady has carried that pain with her all her life, and long after her parents have both died she still carries it. Maybe on that particular day her dad had lost his job, or maybe he was just celebrating with friends. Maybe her father didn't drink as much as his friends. But his drinking that day had caused a lifetime of pain. His behaviour was a problem. I had the pleasure of praying with that lovely old lady, and she gave Christ the chance to heal that wound. She didn't have to tell me; it would have been painful for her to share that intimate story with a complete stranger, but I don't think she had anyone else.

The day my doorbell rang and I opened the door to see Emma and the boys standing there was the most amazing day, and one I will never forget. It was the Easter holiday. The sun was warm and the spring flowers I had planted the previous autumn were out in all their glory. We had been apart for a year and a half, and now, as I helped them unpack their bags, I thought we would be a family again forever. You might think that having lost them, I would treasure every moment and do anything not to lose them again. I was prepared to wash the dishes every night for the rest of my life. I had a second chance, and when you lose something precious, you really understand its value. But something wasn't right.

Where I may have thought they were back for good and that Emma had come back because she loved me, the reality, from her perspective, was very different. Her father had strongly advised against any reconciliation, and she had come back to see if she could trust me again. Could she love me again, despite the things I had done and the lies I had told her for three years of our marriage? Had I known that, and not been so insensitive in my own happiness and delight at our reunion, maybe I would have behaved differently. Maybe I would have been more attuned to her way of thinking and more sensitive to her needs.

It's easy to avoid communication and intimacy when you are the parent of an autistic child. We let Matty dictate the pace and didn't find time to talk or to share our needs and perceptions. The steamroller that is my natural default setting just ploughed on through life. I should have understood that I needed to earn back her trust, and that it would take time. I just assumed she had given it back to me when she moved in again. I assumed that the beautiful garden that had been our marriage, before I became a gambler, would be right there outside our new home together. The reality was that our garden was a barren and empty place, and we needed to plant some new flowers together.

That first evening I took a bottle of champagne out of the fridge. I had been saving it for this occasion. I filled Emma's glass, but when I poured myself a glass and looked up at her face, there was a look of fear in her eyes I will never forget. She was afraid because she thought that, given I had been addicted to gambling, I could easily become addicted to anything, and might drag her and our boys back into misery. I didn't see drinking as one of my issues. But she did. From her perspective, drinking was a problem. Regardless of what I thought about drinking, it had to become a problem from my perspective too. And finally I did stop drinking – for her. But by then it was too late.

When we try to understand our habits and our behaviours, we need to consider the different dimensions, but also the different perspectives.

Some commentators think we all have addictive tendencies, and this may be true. However, I believe that some of us have a greater propensity to addiction than others. But do we all have secret habits, things we like to keep hidden from others? These are habits that may not be full-blown addictions, and may not even be problematic. But we need to be careful that they don't lead to repetitive behaviour that becomes difficult to give up if and when we need to.

I am not trying to make you feel bad. But if your patterns of behaviour cause problems for you or for others, and you are finding it hard to stop or give up, or you fail to meet self-imposed limitation targets, beware. This is something between you and your Maker. The Holy Spirit points out our specific faults; the deceiver makes us feel guilty about everything, all the time, without being specific. We need to be honest about ourselves and live in enough of the light so that our weaknesses and transgressions are exposed for what they are, and not hidden away.

The Recovery Course

The deceiver loves to keep us reliant on things because it spoils our relationships with ourselves, our loved ones, and our God. The modern world provides plenty of opportunities to become hooked on habits.

With a number of wonderfully talented and generous people, I have been leading a Christ-based Recovery Course for the last two years. There are fifteen sessions per course and we have seen some amazing transformations in people's lives as Christ heals them and sets them free. The course follows the twelve steps and puts Christ right back at the heart of recovery. It also shares my understanding that there are spiritual, emotional, and physical elements to addiction, and their respective needs at each level must be addressed.

Often I will stand up in a church to announce the start of a new course, but when I mention the word "addiction" I lose eye contact with my audience, or they stop listening as attentively. I hear the shuffle of feet as they become restless. They check their watches and cough more often. The word "addiction" comes with a huge stigma attached. It conjures up pictures of homeless alcoholics and hopeless drug addicts. Most people, especially those in our church congregations, don't see themselves as addicts. And yet it is believed that 73 per cent of all males in churches across the UK and the USA regularly access pornography on the internet, and that almost a third of the women in our congregations are regularly accessing pornography. Perhaps we would be more honest if we called ourselves addicts when it comes to our use of substances like coffee and sugar that we would find it so hard to live without, or the process of overeating when we feel stressed or in need of comfort.

Let's not get hung up on a word. But we do need to be honest with ourselves. As the father of a disabled child, I know how hard it is to obtain the resources and care he really needs in life. It has been a battle at every turn. But we have had some victories and found that there is wonderful care available. You just have to fight, fight, fight when resources are limited. The first question we were asked when we wanted Matty to see a speech and language therapist, or an occupational therapist, or have a special teacher to assist him at school, was, "Do you have a diagnosis?" When, after a two-year battle, Matty was finally given a written diagnosis for autism (to go with his previously diagnosed epilepsy and hemiplegia), it opened up a whole new world of medical provision. Unless we are ready to admit we have a problem – and yes, that might mean we have to label ourselves with the entire stigma attached – we will not be able to find the recovery and support we need.

I met a newly appointed vicar recently. He told me he wanted to come on The Recovery Course, not as a leader, but to get help with some issues he has around eating. I just wanted to give him a hug and tell him how brave he was. What a shining example he would be. He risked the ridicule and judgment of his congregation by being honest enough to admit he had a problem.

Foundations

Don't worry about labels; just be willing to accept that you may have a problematic habit. I am happy to accept you might want to use the words "secret compulsions" rather than addiction. It really doesn't matter, as long as whatever you come up with allows you the freedom to take it seriously enough to understand that it is causing problems in your life, and that therefore you need help to overcome it.

Whenever I walked past a high street bookmaker's shop, I used to look in and feel sorry for the folk inside. I would compare myself to them thinking, I'm not as bad as them. Then I would probably go home and spend hours online. It's very tempting to justify our behaviour by comparing ourselves with others. This is not about anyone other than you. It's dangerous to justify your own behaviour or substance use based on the perceived behaviour of others. It will either condemn or falsely liberate you. Just take care of your side of the street and let others do the same. The questions in the exercise at the end of this chapter will help you realize where you are, provided you are prepared to be honest. If you are honest and you score well that is great news, you probably don't have a problem, but please beware!

In the Alcoholics Anonymous and Gamblers Anonymous programme, step 1 says, "We admitted we were powerless over our addiction and that our lives had become unmanageable." It doesn't really matter how you label your behaviour as long as you accept you have lost control and your life is being disrupted as a result. If you can accept that, then my dear reader, you have overcome denial, the biggest hurdle to recovery of them all. Step 2 is about believing that Christ can restore you again. It says, "We came to believe that a power greater than ourselves could restore us to sanity." If you can accept that you have a problem you have lost control of and believe that God can restore you, then you have achieved the first two steps. These are the most fundamental of all and provide the foundation for any recovery. If you get that, you are well on your way to recovery. If not, put the book down and come back to it when you are ready to accept the truth.

You might be reading this and not feel ready to admit you have a problem. I wouldn't have been. It took me three years to accept that I had lost control. I left it until I had lost everything and was about to be made homeless. What a great result that was! Maybe if I had found the sense to cry out for help, I wouldn't have lost my wife. Please – if you have the chance – don't make the same mistake that I did. Answer the questions at the end of this chapter as honestly as you can. There is no sequence of answers or a score that will cause a red light to flash and the word "addict" to jump out. The questions are not there to make you feel guilty, but if you have answered honestly and you have prayed that the Holy Spirit will shine a light on all aspects of your life, you may see the truth for the first time.

The truth is we all need recovery from life. We all want freedom; we all need Christ!

Review

The word "addiction" comes with a stigma. Be open to the fact that you have a habit that you are not always in control of, and that it might be causing you or someone else a problem. Don't compare the extent of your habit with others. Turn back to God in the certainty that he can and will return you to sanity.

Exercise

If you don't know whether your habit is just an occasional slip or something more destructive, answer the following questions honestly:

- If you were marooned on a desert island, what would you miss the most?

- What takes up most of your leisure time, and what is it you daydream about most?

- What do you do that gives you the greatest buzz?
- Is there anything you do that you would hate others to witness?
- Are you addicted to something socially acceptable, like your job or your money?
- Does your habit make you unhappy?
- Do you ever feel remorse after you have indulged your habit?
- Has your habit ever caused an argument or conflict at home?
- Have you ever taken time off work because of your habit?
- Has your habit ever caused you to miss a quiet time or church, or interrupted your regular prayer time?
- Does your habit cause a decrease in your efficiency, your ability to plan ahead, or your ambitions?
- Has your habit ever caused you financial concern?
- Have you ever lied to cover up your habit?
- Have you ever lost sleep because of your habit?
- Have you ever set yourself a limit and failed to stick to it?
- Do you find yourself thinking about your habit when you are daydreaming?

  Turn your own will over to the care of God, every morning. Make a prayer list which you can keep to. Pray at home, in the car, on the train, or when you are walking, but also make sure you do it every morning.

CHAPTER 5

Honesty without Masks

A few years ago I had a wardrobe. It was huge. It had to be: inside were all my masks. I had one for every occasion. There were masks for work (one for clients, one for my colleagues, and another for my boss), church, home, socializing, and family gatherings. You name it, the mask was in there. The masks were my protection, something to hide behind when my own face wasn't impressive enough. Not so long ago I called in the removal men and we took a journey to a place called Calvary. There I burnt my wardrobe. And with it all my masks.

If I am really honest, sometimes I miss my wardrobe and all it contained. I recently spoke at the National Mental Health Nursing Conference at the 02 Arena. I had to follow a well-known and hugely popular comedian, whom I knew would entertain and make the delegates laugh, all 2,000 of them. I didn't have any jokes in my repertoire. On the morning of the conference, I put on my best suit and polished my shoes. As I was leaving, I took a quick look at myself in the mirror. Staring back at me, as I rehearsed my lines, was a brand new mask: a red Power Ranger. It took courage to take it off and throw it in the bin. As I drove up to London I thought about the day I had worn a mask for the first time.

The end of innocence

My dad was the rock in my young life. I rarely saw him show any emotion. I guess his father had shown him little either. Looking back, I think it would have helped me more if he had been able to do so. My mother, on the other hand, wore her heart on her sleeve. Dad was there for the serious stuff, like helping with homework or anything financial. He worked long hours to earn enough to give six children a good start in life. Mum was there for fun and games, laughter, and food. I had a very close relationship with her. She was the one who made breakfast, dropped us off at school, collected us, fed us, and made us feel safe. She planned great adventures in the woods that surrounded our house in the country. She made picnics and told us stories that transformed a simple walk into a grand treasure hunt on a desert island. She was there to nurse me back to health when I was sick.

By the time I was thirteen, I guess my teachers would have called me well adjusted. I enjoyed my own company and would happily spend time playing in the garden on my own. But I also enjoyed the company of others and had been taught to be polite, well mannered, and grateful to adults. My grades at school were good enough to cause cautious optimism that I might achieve something in life. I was also one of the best swimmers for my age group in the country.

I had a wonderful, carefree childhood, enveloped by the knowledge that I was loved by my mother. I knew my mother was proud of me when I won my races on sports day at school. But I also knew I was loved when I came last, or when I was the only child in my class not to be invited to a birthday party, and when I fell off my bike and broke my finger so badly it had to be reset. As we waited in the hospital reception to have an X-ray for one bone or another, when asked if we had been there before, my mother recited the dates and bones for which I had been X-rayed before as though she were reciting battle honours at a remembrance parade.

I was loved, and with it came security and the freedom to be myself. I don't think I would have liked wearing a mask; I'm sure I would have found it uncomfortable, too tight, and would have stopped me from seeing clearly or breathing properly.

But one night, all that changed.

My homework was finished, my school bag was packed and ready for the morning, and my school uniform was hanging neatly on the back of my door. Swimming training had been particularly tough that evening and I knew I would be back in the pool for an hour before I even left for school the following day.

I was ready for sleep, but as I felt myself drifting off there was a gentle knock on my bedroom door. "Just, I need to talk to you."

He didn't put the light on, but there was enough light from the landing for me to see that his cheeks were wet from tears and his eyes puffy and red. "I've just come from the hospital. I said goodbye to your mother. The doctors don't expect her to make it through the night. They've given her a new drug that she may respond to, but they told me to prepare for the worst. I am telling you and your sister because you are both teenagers now and you are old enough to know."

With those words, my childhood ended. I cried for most of the night. In the morning I discovered I now shared my life with a new character, one equipped with a highly attuned defence mechanism. He showed me all the beautiful masks he kept neatly packed away in a big wardrobe.

My mother didn't die, but that night I glimpsed the fragility of life. I came to understand that what I had so innocently taken for granted could leave at any stage. The ones we love the most could abandon us, either deliberately or by misfortune.

The new person gave me comfort from the pain I felt. The new person showed me how to protect myself from the pain of loss by hiding behind a perfect mask. He helped me cope with the sudden and shocking realization that I might at any time be abandoned by people I had been so blind to have loved.

My mother did not die; she made a full and quite miraculous recovery six years later. But the damage had been done. By the morning I had already become friends with my new self. This self meant that acceptance, popularity, and an unquenchable desire to be liked by anyone and everyone I met became all consuming. If I could be liked by everyone, not all of them could abandon me and I would always have someone who loved me. There would be safety in numbers.

At first my new self, an outwardly confident lad, was only there some of the time, but soon, fuelled by the insecurities of teenage life, he became my dominant personality. He was a loud, limelight-stealing imposter, with an insatiable desire to be loved, to be liked, and to be the centre of attention. I wanted to be the schoolboy every mother wished their own son could be, the one the boys all wanted to be friends with and the girls all wanted to kiss at Christmas and write silly poems about. During the years when my mother was ill, I was passed from home to home, staying for several weeks with one well-meaning family, only to be moved on again to another. This just served to highly attune the defence mechanisms of my other self and to set him to work even harder at being successful, in the hope that the new family would like me enough to want me to stay longer than a few weeks.

My old self, a meek, happy youngster, content to play on his own and take joy in the simple company of others, withered and was replaced by an alter ego who needed constant reassurance of his validity through achievement and praise. I threw myself at any competitive situation, patted myself on the back when I swam ever faster and set new records in an insatiable desire for medals and accolades. As I stood on the top of the podium week after week, my new self provided the assurance I craved from others. I volunteered for everything, made the top rank in the air cadets, and even persuaded my teachers to let me take my exams early so I could study more subjects and pass more exams. I trained twice a day in the pool and competed up and down the country, as well as internationally most weekends. I was desperate to please my coaches, my teachers, and anyone in authority. Something had to give.

And then I was rejected by a beautiful girl in my final year at school. With this rejection, my world came off its tracks, and I began to realize that maybe the world didn't love me as I had thought it did. The side of my character that had offered me comfort from the pain had lied to me and pretended it had the answer. It had said, "Don't be yourself because the world won't like you as you are. Achieve and it will love you again. And when you can't achieve, pretend."

So was laid a blueprint for my life that gave me some huge success, but also robbed me of the security of being myself, of being content to just be me. I was restless, unsettled, unless I was receiving adoration from my peers or love from a girl. It led me to treat some lovely, kind girls in a shameful and quite cruel way. I didn't even know how to love myself, but still I pretended I could offer them love and affection, when all I was doing, in reality, was affirming my sense of being liked, using them to feed my sense of security as they fell for me. Once they professed their love, I would callously move on in search of someone else.

When I was seventeen I attended a Bible week and came back to church full of "the Holy Spirit". I was determined to start a new youth group and convert everyone in my classes at school. When the minister, very wisely, told me to sleep on my young ministry, I dismissed him as lacking in faith and turned my back on that church to find another that would be able to accommodate my massive calling – and ego. Often I would try to find a church with the best-looking girls so I could impress them with my "spirituality". I was a fake.

A few years later, I had found a career in the army which allowed me opportunities to succeed and gain the respect and adoration of my fellow officers, my juniors, and my seniors. Failing my flying training hurt, as we will see, but I soon found another regiment. As long as there was another girl, a new challenge, a new opportunity to succeed, I was OK – or I told myself I was OK, which at that point amounted to the same thing. I had the opportunity to prove myself in the army. I rocketed to the rank of major at the earliest opportunity, but when I watched my friends catch up and even overtake me, I turned my back on the army and headed for the city, once more to prove myself.

The false person, the person I displayed in all its finery like a cock pheasant in breeding season, was now so much a part of me that I was convinced it was me. I didn't even realize I wasn't being honest with myself or those around me.

I was driving a car that was all show on the outside, but if you were to lift the bonnet, the engine was rusty, the wires were frayed, and the fuel pipes were blocked. I was like a kit car with fine spoilers, metallic paint, and alloy wheels. It had double exhaust pipes that made a reassuringly loud noise when I put my foot on the accelerator, not because it had power, but because the pipes had rusted through.

The needs of the false persona leave an emptiness that can never be filled, but it was one I tried to fill with people. Anthony DeMellow in *The Way to Love* describes the result of this futile behaviour pattern, how we can allow people to control our behaviour by their approval or disapproval. In this way, they can ease our loneliness, send our spirits soaring with their praise, or bring us "down to the depths with their criticism and rejection". He goes on to suggest that we spend our time placating and pleasing people, living or dead. We conform to their standards, seek their company, desire their love, dread their ridicule, long for their applause, and submit to the guilt they lay upon us. We fear ridicule so we resort to conformity. We fear rejection so we try to make ourselves more likeable. In short, we are enslaved by others. That was how it was for me until I met Emma.

Married bliss

Meeting Emma temporarily silenced my extroverted self. She loved me unconditionally. I had also achieved enough success at work to silence my need to keep proving myself. I suddenly found I was content to just be. I lived, for a time, in the moment, happy to be a father and a husband. But my Mount Vesuvius was still there, and the part of me that had dominated for almost three decades was not happy at being put to sleep. When Matty almost died, and when I was passed over for promotion, I did something really stupid. I was still carrying pain, and although at rest, the tiger inside me had not stopped growing. Maybe I wanted to test the depth of Emma's love for me; maybe I needed to be convinced that she would not abandon me. I don't recall hearing a clear voice, but looking back, maybe my other self, my deceiver – or, as Brennan Manning so eloquently calls it, the "imposter" – convinced me Emma would abandon me when love wore off and I revealed my true self.

Gambling became the place I went in secret to prove my worth. The problem with gambling is that the cards are stacked in favour of the table. If you gamble enough you will lose in the long run. I never accepted defeat as a reason to stop. It drove me to complete destruction. If I wanted to see if Emma would abandon me, I found out. After three years of my self-indulgence, deceit, gluttony of waste, and insanity, Emma was right to leave.

The Swiss psychiatrist, Carl Jung, talks about the shadow personality, all the bits of our character we hide from ourselves and others. If I am honest, I think that at the end of my three-year gambling binge, my life was mostly made up of my shadow personality. The bit I tried to display outwardly was just a sliver of what was left. My life was a lie, and I was self-destructing. I didn't even know the real Justyn. Maybe the real Justyn died at the age of thirteen.

At the end I had a choice. I could take my own sorry life, the cowardly way out; or I could face up to my demons, and either walk the streets or live back home with my mother.

Humbled and set free

I chose to come home. And that night, in complete humiliation, as I have said, with my pride totally gone, I got down on my knees and I prayed a simple prayer.

I said I was sorry. I asked Christ to mend me, to come back into my heart again. It was the last day I placed a bet. He forgave me – although it took a while for me to forgive myself – and he mended me, from the inside. He did it in a very simple way and it took a while. The destructive habit of gambling ended there and then, but he had to deal with my volcano, my other self, the imposter.

On 17 August 2013, five and a half million people woke up and read a story about an ex-army major who gambled three-quarters of a million pounds in three years and lost everything as a result.

When I opened the double-page spread and saw the picture of myself staring back at me, I was horrified. My other self screamed, "You fool! Now the whole world will know what you are really like. An idiot who lost everything by your own stupidity."

Those were the last words I clearly heard from my other self. That day, after thirty years of running amok, my Creator put him to sleep. The article meant I had no need to pretend any more. My faults were exposed.

My overwhelming emotion that day was fear. Fear that I would be rejected by society as a loser, a misfit. But as I began to receive messages of encouragement from people who had read the article, I realized that Christ had indeed set me free. I was free to be myself: a flawed person with many faults, but completely loved in spite of them, and totally forgiven by a God whose grace has no limits. That knowledge of unconditional love made me realize I would never be abandoned. I couldn't lose that love. Just as importantly, I couldn't earn it or make it any greater by my own actions.

Some messages were from people who had been gambling in private and the article had given them the confidence to confront the issue. Other messages came in from wives worried about husbands, or parents worried about children. They asked for advice or simply said thank you. There was even a message from a couple who said the article saved their marriage.

> *My old self has been crucified with Christ. It is no longer I who live, but Christ lives in me. So I live in this earthly body by trusting in the Son of God, who loved me and gave himself for me.*
>
> **Galatians 2:20**

It is this perfect truth of Jesus' love for me as he allowed himself to be crucified on my behalf that allowed my old self to die.

Once I measured my worth by my success, my popularity, my annual reports, my salary, my promotions, my ability to beat the odds and win a bet... the list is endless. It meant I would never be quite worthy enough. In overcoming my fear of what others would think of me, by publicly sharing my story, God set me free. When my old self died, I began to see myself as God sees me: not perfect, but forgiven and deeply loved; his son, his beloved one.

My identity stopped being drawn from my achievements, from the perceptions of others. Or worse, from my own perception of how I thought others perceived me. That gave me, and goes on giving me, the freedom to be myself. It broke the shackles of the need to be appreciated, recognized, and respected. My self-respect came from a simple appreciation for the everyday. I had a sense of existing in the here and now, and understanding my place in a created world where I was loved infinitely by a God who enjoyed my company.

I didn't have all the answers, but the questions didn't matter any more. God was as real to me as the ground I stood on. My belief became a certainty that transformed my outlook on life, shook up my priorities, and gave me a hope and purpose. It gave me the true identity I had been searching for in shadows and weak reflections.

I didn't have a sense of arriving, a spiritual awakening, just a profound certainty that things were right and that this new intimacy was just the beginning. I knew that it could and would grow, becoming deeper as I became more like the one I loved, each day more intimate. I also knew it would only end on the day I looked my Creator in the eyes and he could tell me to my face, "My dear son, I have loved you from the moment you were conceived and I have always known you. Now come and spend eternity with me in my home."

We need to define ourselves in Christ, as he sees us. Not as we think he sees us, but as beloved children of God. Any other identity is false, an optical illusion, as though we have taken the blue pill in *The Matrix*. Not that the imposter doesn't fight back on occasion. Sometimes when I open an email from someone who has read my book, or seen me on TV, I hear a little voice, if I strain to listen. The little voice compliments me on how well I am doing, on how much hope I'm bringing to people. But then, every time I stand up in front of a group of people and share my story, or go on the radio and talk about the madness of my addiction, I am reminded of my weaknesses, my frailty, and my imperfections. Then the voice goes quiet. I don't hate myself or even dislike myself, but I don't have an over-inflated opinion of myself either. Through grace, I see myself as Christ sees me: flawed, but loved.

Often I am asked how I found recovery, what was my recovery pathway? Was it cognitive behavioural therapy, professional counselling, or prolonged abstinence? I love it most if I am asked this question on live radio or TV because I know my answer can't be edited out. I always say, "I have found lasting recovery by a realization of the truth, that I am loved unconditionally by Christ. That's not to say cognitive behaviour therapy doesn't work. I know it has helped a huge number of people. But, as a Christian, I believe in the power of Christ and the healing he has for us, either in the short, medium or long term.

The benefits of honesty

It was the honesty of telling the truth about what happened that freed me from the grip of a pretend persona. A lack of honesty and too much fear are the two fundamental issues that prevent us from accepting the gift of freedom and recovery from our secret and compulsive habits. But that honesty is very much tied into denial. Denial is the biggest preventer of recovery.

If you know you have a habit you are ashamed of, but you are not prepared to be totally honest with yourself, or you are thinking, "This is really interesting, but I have everything under control," then please put this book down. You are wasting your time reading it. Honesty will be the foundation upon which you build your recovery. You will need to be honest with yourself, honest with those closest to you, and honest with God. And since, "The time is coming when everything that is covered up will be revealed, and all that is secret will be made known to all" (Luke 12:2), you may as well just 'fess up and get it over with. Dishonesty will hold you up and prevent recovery. Dishonesty leads to denial. It perpetuates your habit, justifies your behaviour, and stops you from realizing you have a problem and getting the help you need.

In short, a lack of honesty, when it comes to recovery, is bad. Very bad. I apologize to those of you who are reading this thinking, "I wish he would stop banging on about denial. I know I have a problem; I just want to know how to get fixed." It's just that I know this was my biggest issue. I accepted I had a problem, but I still convinced myself I could handle it, and anyway, the consequences of asking for help and owning up would lead to far more problems. The problem is that until we accept that we can't do it on our own, things will only get worse, so when it finally does come out, there is a far bigger problem.

I guess, if I am honest, that no amount of anyone telling me this would have made a difference. I just don't want anyone to experience what was the worst day of my life, when it all came crashing down. In retrospect, I wish I had been honest a lot earlier.

In *The Ragamuffin Gospel*, Brennan Manning talks about the importance of honesty in terms of secret habits:

> *Honesty is such a precious commodity that is seldom found in the world or the church. Honesty requires the truthfulness to admit the attachment and the addictions that control our attention, to dominate our consciousness, and function as false gods. I can be addicted to vodka or being nice, to marijuana or being loved, to cocaine or being right, to gambling or relationships, to golf or gossiping. Perhaps my addiction is food, performance, money, popularity, power, revenge, reading, television, tobacco, weight or winning. When we give anything more priority than we give to God, we commit idolatry.*[3]

He goes on to say that honesty is harder, but also more important when we have accepted God's grace. This is because we have to face the truth of who we are, even if the reality is not pleasant. It means being truthful about our secret habits, recognizing the things we avoid and also the things we cling to in a less-than-healthy way. Manning makes the point that regular self-confrontation takes strength and courage, and we will fail frequently. The good news is that we are not alone. As we go deeper into our relationship with God, it is our Helper, the Holy Spirit, who holds up a mirror to our true selves and allows us to see where we are wrong, but also encourages us and gives us joy when we get it right, when we make the right choices.

If we are really honest and not pretending to be a spiritual superstar or even just saying we are fine when we hurt, then, and only then, do we open ourselves to the opportunity to receive God's grace, to the inflow of his forgiveness and healing. Pretence blocks recovery because it's not honest enough to admit we are weak.

I wasn't honest with myself. I had lost sight of my inner self, the real one, and concentrated on the outside, my shell, my demeanour,

---

3   Brennan Manning, *The Ragamuffin Gospel* (Authentic, 1990).

the bit people see but don't know, the part they judge but don't understand, so I could deceive them into thinking I was a certain kind of person. I was scared that they might see me as I was and somehow reject me or not love me.

We all put on a bit of a show: make-up, new clothes, the car we drive, and the things we drop into conversations. They are all types of mask. I am not saying it's always wrong to do that. For many of us, our masks are a way of protecting ourselves. I know mine were. But wouldn't it be better if we could just be honest enough to be who we are without that fear of rejection? That's surely what Christ wants for us.

As we become more comfortable within ourselves, we find more happiness, more peace, and more joy; we are able to appreciate the present and not regret the past or hanker for the future, to live in the here and now. To God, your face is beautiful. Don't hide it from him. Don't think for one minute that you can create something more beautiful than he already has.

One of the things I used to yearn for as I came off an eight-hour betting spree (I could last for as long as my bank balance lasted, often through the night, sometimes for two days and nights), was a walk in the woods, some fresh air, genuine laughter with my wife, or a game with my children. When we are comfortable in the company of our true self, without make-up or a mask, we can appreciate the simple things around us: sounds, smells and tastes, and, above all, other people. Accepting who we really are and not disliking ourselves means we are better placed to love other people, which is what we are commanded to do (John 13:34). It's funny, but I have come to notice that as I draw closer to God, I become more relaxed, more at peace, more comfortable in my own company. I also enjoy music more and walks in the countryside!

The deception is that we actually believe we need the reassurance of our possessions, our wealth, the approval of people we meet, the number of likes we get on Facebook, or the number of followers we have on Twitter. These things will never satisfy our inner need to be loved and accepted, so we seek solace in ensnaring habits; we hunt down pleasure for comfort and try to fill the void. In doing so we get further away from our inner self because those habits drag us down and lower our self-esteem; they do the complete opposite to the purpose we intended in the first place. What's even worse is that they are habit forming, so in the end we end up doing them without even knowing why. It's a destructive cycle.

God is a genuine God; he's not so interested in the outside. It is only when we accept his gift of perfect love that we begin to feel satisfied and fulfilled. He made us that way. The hard part for us humans is to understand that we are loved for who we are. Addiction and any secret habit robs us of our self-esteem. Our habit becomes a self-fulfilling source of self-hatred and self-loathing. If we can't love or even like ourselves, how can we accept God's love – or anyone else's, for that matter?

Jesus was the only man who was genuine in every situation. When we find intimacy in our relationship with Jesus, when we become more like him by walking more closely with him, listening to him through his word, allowing the Holy Spirit to transform us, and doing lovely things rather than just talking about them, he goes right to our inner self, our genuine true and real self, and offers us the love we need to set us free to be real. To be comfortable, to just be us. And in the reassurance of this love, we can love others and enjoy real relationships that build up and don't pull down. We need constructive, not destructive, relationships.

Honesty at church

When it comes to our secret habits, honesty among Christians is tough. Our God is a God of compassion and forgiveness; he is not judgmental and condemning. And yet, in the very place where we worship him, we are unable to confess our weaknesses and our faults to each other for fear of being judged. How many times has the Lord spoken to you during a service, but when you hear a call to come forward for prayer, you shrink into your seat, too scared of what people might think if you go up to the front for prayer ministry?

It's often at church that we have the widest and most elaborate range of masks. We fear losing our ministry, or that our brothers and sisters will judge us, or that we won't be invited to lead parts of the church service. We will be shunned and ignored, and looked down upon. Do you go to church because you can't wait to worship your Creator, or is there a tiny element of not wanting people to think you are less than holy if you miss a week? Do you adjust your conversation, ever so slightly, when you talk to your pastor at the end of the service? Do you just happen to mention the fact that you witnessed to a taxi driver on your way home from work during the week?

I constantly need to watch out that my own desire to do good isn't just a sham desire for self-esteem. T. S. Eliot said that the greatest sin is to do the right thing for the wrong reason. We find it so hard to share our weaknesses, cultivating the image that we are saintly warriors for Christ. Could it be that your own church fellowship is so pious you aren't allowed to be a sinner? Or perhaps you just fear the reaction to your honesty. God is not so concerned with the reasons; he just wants us to be free to be ourselves. We are called to be accountable:

Confess your sins to each other and pray for each other so that you may be healed.

James 5:16

Confessing our sins to each other and praying for each other helps in the process of healing and restoration. The second part of this verse talks about the power of a righteous person producing "wonderful results". Our brothers and sisters at church should be the first people we turn to, not the last. I can hear the excuses.

You're saying, "They won't understand," and, "They've never done what I've done," or, "If I tell, everyone will know."

I believe you'll find great compassion and understanding, and if the people you talk to are half as honest as you, your friends at church are probably struggling with similar issues, or have done at some point. When things in our lives are kept hidden in the shadows, they become dangerously destructive and can enjoy a free run. When we bring them out into the light, we are set free because they have no place left to hide.

Don't think for a minute that I'm suggesting you have to stand up and give your testimony at the family service. Just find someone you can trust to keep a confidence and be totally honest with, then open up, bare all, and unburden yourself. The first person I ever told the whole of my story to, from start to finish, is an elder at my church. What a relief it was as he smiled at me, didn't judge me, and just suggested some practical help. He also prayed for me there and then.

In his book *Life Together*, Dietrich Bonhoeffer states that "he who is alone with his sin is utterly alone"[4]. If we are alone, we become accountable only to ourselves. For me, that meant the deceiver had permission to lie to me and prevent me from being honest. My pride stopped me from putting up my hand for help, and the result, in quite a short time, was not at all pretty. When we hide our sins and secret habits, it's easier for the deceiver to justify them. When we pull down the blinds, we become blind. We are on the slippery slope to deceiving ourselves that we are without sin.

If we claim we have no sin, we are only fooling ourselves and not living in the truth.

1 John 1:8

---

4   Dietrich Bonhoeffer, *Life Together* (1939).

Addicted to love

Not living in the truth causes stress and conflict. I have already explained what that can lead to, but we will look at a few causes of stress and conflict in the next part of this book: how they feed our secret habits and how our habits feed stress and conflict, in an ever-reinforcing loop. Our secret habits will remain with us unless we bring our shadow personality into the light and accept that we wear masks. Only then can the cycle be broken. Being accountable to each other achieves this.

I regularly receive messages from people who realize they have reached the end of the line. They know they can't go on with their addiction any longer, but they will say, "I can't tell my husband; he'll leave me." Or, "I can't tell my dad; he will throw me out."

I didn't tell Emma about my habit. She found out. Because she found out I lost all the trust she ever had in me. It takes years to win back trust, and sometimes it never returns. So I generally encourage people to confess, to own up and talk it through with someone they can trust. If the news is all bleak it can be hurtful and possibly harmful to our loved ones, so it's worth taking a few positive steps first, such as seeking counselling, blocking unhealthy websites, joining an Anonymous fellowship, or at least sharing with your pastor: anything that will give hope and demonstrate to your loved ones that you are taking steps to tackle the issue. Don't let them find out before you break the news. You will be scared, but take some positive steps and deliver some hope. Pray first. Pray, pray, and then pray some more. Then just sit down and get it over with. It's quite likely that the person you are telling already knows or at least suspects you have a habit you are hiding.

One day I woke up and realized Christ loves me despite, not because. I understood I had sought love from anyone and everyone I met. And yet I was blind to the one who truly loved me without strings. The truth is this:

We know how much God loves us, and we have put our trust in his love. God is love, and all who live in love live in God, and God lives in them.

1 John 4:16

We are addicted to the wrong kind of love: love for this world, the love we receive from others, the love of pleasure, and the love of money. We need to become addicted to God. We all need to become addicts.

Even as I write this, I can hear a faint voice: "Justyn, don't go all psychological on me now; you're a bloke. Blokes don't do deep."

I am a bloke, but real blokes can be honest. They should be, because without honesty we can't start to recover. When I am at my most genuine, I don't feel the need to wear a mask. When I realize God really loves me, it dawns on me that his love is so much more important than being loved by anything in this world. It gives me the security to face the world just as I am.

If any of these words on honesty resonate with you in any way, but you still keep a few masks tucked away, keep turning your arms over, keep taking those strokes. Don't feel gloomy or disillusioned. Don't feel guilty or condemned. We use masks for our protection. The wonderful news is that when we are assured of God's love, we no longer need to hide. We don't need our masks. We don't need to be scared, even when we go into battle.

Review

God made our faces as they are. He loves to see your face. He doesn't think any of our masks are more attractive than the face he gave you; not even close. Until you are honest with yourself, with others, and with God, recovery and healing are much harder. But it is a process, and one that can take time.

Exercise

- Write down your habits. (Take your time. It may take a day or two to compile the list. Make sure you ask the Holy Spirit to reveal them all.)

- Make a note next to each to mark off the ones you are in control of, the ones that are controlling you, and the ones which can, at times, be a bit of both.

- For the ones which control you, talk to someone. It may be your partner or a friend you trust. Agree to become accountable to them for these issues and ask them to pray for you. This will be hard, but incredibly rewarding!

- Some habits are good for you, like your morning quiet time or your exercise. Make a note of the good habits too.

CHAPTER 6

Recognize it is a Spiritual Battle

For we are not fighting against flesh-and-blood enemies, but against evil rulers and authorities of the unseen world, against mighty powers in this dark world, and against evil spirits in the heavenly places.

Ephesians 6:12

No amount of training could have prepared me for what lay ahead. After ten hours in the water my arms became weak. Darkness fell, and with it my body temperature. At the worst possible time, the wind picked up from a two-knot breeze to a steady fifteen knots. It blew in the opposite direction to the heavy tide, whipping up the sea and tossing me about like a shirt in the wash. Physically I had little left. I had to use my mind, my will, and my emotions to push myself on, even when it hurt, even when the thought of giving up grew stronger and stronger.

In preparation for the swim, I had taken any and every opportunity to talk to Channel swimmers, to ask them what helped them most. Often they would tell me about nutrition and feeding patterns, about not panicking when you get a jellyfish tentacle across your face, or they would advise me to take only cold showers for a year and to sleep with the window open to help acclimatize my body. But the one thing they all agreed on was that when it came down to it, the swim would be 35 per cent physical and 65 per cent in the mind. I didn't really appreciate that until ten hours into it. I was in sight of the French coast but battling against a tide that swept me out to sea, round the part of the French coast I was meant to land on, back out and along the coast towards Belgium. I had to use my mind to override what my body was telling me to do.

I want to make it clear that our battle against addiction, compulsions, or our secret destructive habits is not fought on one dimension. We are engaged in a spiritual battle against dark and unseen powers. The devil is sitting pretty. He knows we are human and knows our weaknesses. He disguises the destructive habits and all the associated sins that go with them, packaging them up with gold paper and tying them with a ribbon. He is the deceiver. These habits look so enticing, so alluring, so innocent. If we accept the truth and see through the deception, we are promised a way out and a great victory.

The temptations in your life are no different from what others experience. And God is faithful. He will not allow the temptation to be more than you can stand. When you are tempted, he will show you a way out so that you can endure.

1 Corinthians 10:13

We need to remember that it's not God who is tempting us, although there have been times in my life when I know he has tested me in order to strengthen my faith. We should also remember that Christ has been through temptation as well and has shown us the way to gain victory. We can overcome temptation by wearing the armour of God.

We should accept that our battle against our secret habits is not just a physical battle, although for many addictions there is a very strong physical or chemical element. The battle is fought on spiritual and emotional planes as well. Our habits are often the symptom of an underlying emotional pain or hurt. Facing up to this pain, even when we don't know it's there, is hard; it goes against our natural instinct. Our minds don't like the fear, the embarrassment, the shame, the emptiness, the loneliness, or the conflict. So we reach for our medication, our drug of choice to anaesthetize, to soothe the open wound.

This inner hurt needs to be dealt with to achieve long-term recovery. I mean fully dealt with, not just lanced, drained, or patched up, but surgically removed. Anything else, any other recovery model, therapy, or treatment is just like sticking a plaster over a deep gash that needs antiseptic and stitches. But how can we do this? How can we identify and then remove a pain, resentment, or hurt that may have been with us all our lives, or maybe one we can't even see?

I believe, without any hesitation, that the very best way to deal with the pain is to let Christ change us from within. So there is a spiritual dimension which must take precedence over any physical or emotional one. We have to change the way we think, act, and process our environment. Otherwise we will never truly find long-term and lasting recovery. That can only come from a change within our hearts. To achieve freedom from being dragged down into the gutter of our habits and all the damage they cause to relationships, careers, health, and financial stability, we have to accept that we need a multidimensional approach. If we allow Christ to deal with our inner pain, it reduces or eliminates our emotional need to medicate. With our emotions dealt with, our habits become purely physical issues which can be dealt with by way of a few techniques like knowing and avoiding triggers and putting in blocks.

I don't have all the answers; I have had to learn this the hard way myself. I thought I could just ask God to heal me there and then, and my physical cravings would cease. I did, and the cravings did stop, but there was so much more Christ needed to do in my life to make me content, at peace, and in tune with life. Recovery shouldn't just be long, agonizing day after day of abstinence, or fighting a battle not to do something that you really want to do. True freedom means not even thinking about your old way of life, not being able to conceive that the old you would have used your drug of choice!

Twelve steps to recovery

The fact that overcoming addiction requires us to adopt a multidimensional approach was recognized by Bill Wilson and others when they designed the twelve-step approach to recovery from alcoholism in the 1930s.

The twelve steps are spiritual steps, and at their very heart is the fundamental truth that only through God can we find true and lasting recovery. The steps have been criticized, mostly by non-Christians or those who don't believe in God. This is probably because the critics don't believe there are three dimensions to recovery, and so tend to place the emphasis on the physical or more tangible dimension. It is possible to "white knuckle" recovery, to abstain by sheer willpower. Contrary to common belief, addicts have tremendous willpower. When it comes to feeding our habit, we can be exceptionally resourceful and devious. But recovery by this method is not easy and, I would argue, not sustainable in the long or even medium term. That's why I see so many people returning to Gamblers Anonymous (GA) meetings after a three-month or a six-month break, or even after one, two, or three years.

The steps have helped many people, and the chapters in this book follow loosely the sequence of the spiritual steps. We have already covered the first two steps: avoiding denial and confessing our situation to God. I know that there are other ways to find recovery than using the steps. It's not the steps that hold the power to heal, fix, and restore. That power is in Christ. The steps are just one way of allowing the power of Christ to heal.

GA helped me massively, particularly in the early stages when I finally overcame my denial and sought help. I realized I wasn't alone. But I was also troubled by not being able to talk freely about what, for me, was the fundamental key to my recovery: the realization of the truth that I was loved by God. Not just a higher power of choice, but my Creator. A Creator who made me and wants me to be free.

I also felt quite gloomy at the idea that I would have to attend the meetings for the rest of my life or risk slipping back into my old ways. I believe that, through Christ, we can and are set free, once and for all. There is no life sentence. That's not to say I can ever be complacent about my own recovery. I still need to take stock each day and I recognize that I can never, ever place a bet again without risk of my whole life imploding. I can't buy a lottery ticket, not even a raffle ticket – and don't ever ask me for a sportsman's bet on a golf course! The twelve-step programme can never be completed and then forgotten as we move into our new happy life of freedom. The last three steps, as we will see, are known as "the maintenance steps". They are steps, or perhaps a better description would be "simple daily actions", that we take each day to maintain our recovery and avoid our natural instinct to slip back into our old behaviour patterns.

I want to emphasize here that there is a danger of *only* seeing our addiction in the spiritual dimension. There are also both physical and emotional aspects, and these need to be taken care of. The danger of seeing addiction only as a spiritual issue is that we then don't take responsibility for our actions. We can't just expect our recovery to fall into our lap. Christ can and does heal dramatically, but we don't have a divine right to expect to be suddenly healed without first taking steps to choose not to use. My own recovery, through Christ, was there waiting for me at any stage during my three years of abuse. I only had to ask for it. But that's just it. We have to ask, and when we ask we have to want it.

If we also recognize that our habits are not just physical, we are one step closer to recovery. We are closer to identifying and using the most appropriate methods of striking back at the fortresses that have become our addictions and habits and not just putting a plaster over a gaping wound. "We use God's mighty weapons, not worldly weapons, for the destruction of fortresses" (2 Corinthians 10:4).

The news today was full of faraway battles as well as some much closer to home in the city streets we once felt safe to walk.

77

I have seen at first hand the devastation of a battleground and the aftermath of ethnic cleansing. It's not something I ever want to experience again. But the key battleground against evil is even closer: it's within ourselves. And it doesn't look like a war-torn city; it looks like a warm, cosy bar, filled with attractive, seemingly happy people. Once we recognize this we are a step closer to overcoming our secret habits.

> *Resist the devil, and he will flee from you. Come close to God, and God will come close to you.*
>
> **James 4:7–8**

Knowing this simple truth will help you stop giving in to the urge you have to use. It will also help you avoid slipping up once you are well on your way. Even when you are bruised and see no light at the end of the tunnel, when you realize the enormity of the damage you have done, you can still call out to God. You just need to be broken enough to realize what you are doing is wrong, and that you are not God. You can't fix it on your own. I had to fall a long way before I realized this truth, so please don't think I'm saying this is easy. It's not.

> *He will not crush the weakest reed,*
> *or put out a flickering candle.*
>
> **Isaiah 42:3**

For some, it's that easy. Just call out to our heavenly Father. But the hardest part is to get to the point where we realize we need help, when we suddenly see the reality of what we're doing, that it is both destructive and hurtful. It may be much easier for those around you to see your problem, and they may desperately want you to get help, but until you are ready to get help, until you are ready to bend your knee and turn your back on what you may not even be willing to recognize as a problem, you won't find recovery.

For those of you with loved ones who you know are self-destructing, you can't ever make someone get help until they are ready. They need to submit, acknowledge the issue, and seek help themselves. You can't do that for them. I know it's hard. Watching me self-destruct was, my mother has told me, one of the hardest things she has ever had to do. She has only recently come off the medication she was prescribed to help her through it!

If it was as easy as just confessing, we wouldn't be suffering in the way we all do, addicts and their loved ones alike. The problem is that the enemy is a master of disguise. We often don't recognize the problem until it's too late, and even then we have to overcome our fear of admitting the problem to others and battle through denial before we even seek help.

By the way, if your habit has a hold of you and you feel ashamed of it, please don't keep it to yourself, thinking, I'm too ashamed to tell anyone. Can't I just ask God to help me and we can just keep it to ourselves, and when I'm fixed there'll be no need to tell anyone? Or maybe when I'm fixed, I can share my testimony about how God and I overcame a bad habit.

My honest advice is to share it now, while it's at its worst. Talking about it out loud means it becomes more tangible, something you can't ignore or put off any more.

The hidden things that trip us

The modern world is packed full of hidden things that trip us and distract us from our primary purpose in life, which is to enjoy an intimate relationship with God. We have so many things that distract: the things that glitter, things that everybody is doing, things that look like fun. I heard recently that, on average, young people process more information in one day than their great-grandparents would have done in a month.

We are bombarded by advertising that tells us how to look,

ONE DAY AT A TIME

how to behave, what to do, what to wear, and who to like. When we inevitably fall short of this standard we can't help feeling inadequate. Gambling advertising, which has increased by 1,400 per cent in the UK since reforms to the Gambling Act in 2007, tells us at all hours of the day that it is good to gamble our money; it's fun and rewarding. As a result, 560,000 are addicted, with a further 3.5 million at risk. More than one million of us in the UK struggle with anorexia and bulimia, while compulsive eating, which is often a result of anxiety, is the predominant cause of 15 million people becoming obese. Facebook, Twitter, and other forms of social media are a breeding ground for compulsive behaviour. The condition Facebook Addiction Disorder (FAD) is now a recognized affliction causing the breakdown of marriages and other misery. Thirty per cent of all those who drink go on to develop some form of problem or dependency, and the most affected demographic are women over the age of 50. I haven't even mentioned the internet and all its associated problems.

The extortionately priced packets of cigarettes now come with health warnings, but that doesn't stop one in three adults in the UK from putting their lives at risk. So just imagine how deceptive our other habits can be, the ones that don't come with such obvious health warnings. Society often accepts and encourages addiction and turns a blind eye. We might even joke about being a workaholic. And yet these habits can be equally as destructive to our health, our relationships, and even our sanity.

Today's battles

I served in the army for more than eight years. By the time I was leaving at the turn of the century, a new method of warfare was developing rapidly: PSYOPS, or Psychological Operations, which the US Department of Defense defines as:

Planned operations to convey selected information and indicators to foreign audiences to influence their emotions, motives, objective reasoning, and ultimately the behaviour of foreign governments, organizations, groups, and individuals. The purpose of psychological operations is to induce or reinforce foreign attitudes and behaviour favourable to the originator's objectives.

The doctrine has been developed by highly skilled psychologists under the banner of "perception management". Stealth technology and deception are also employed in the modern battlefield.

Without a doubt, we are subject to some perception management warfare. The devil wants to influence our attitudes to achieve his objectives. That's what addiction is, in a nutshell.

I first trained as a soldier in the latter stages of the Cold War. We knew our enemy; we knew where and how "the Red Bear" would deploy. We even rehearsed it over and over again. Imagine a fully equipped army, with all the latest technology and equipment, poised and ready to deploy. Thirty years ago it would have been clear who the enemy was. They would be forming up on the border ready to invade. Now, with the explosion of global terrorism, our foe might look just like anyone else sitting on a train or drinking at a bar. The truth is, any fully equipped and highly trained army is rendered worthless if their enemy is just a radicalized trained pilot who manages to fly an aircraft into the heart of a city. Warfare may be a poor analogy, but wherever you sit politically, please recognize that our fight against addiction is a spiritual battle against the spiritual realms.

The devil is the ultimate deceiver, so we need to be aware of where he will attack by knowing ourselves better. We must become aware of our points of weakness and recognize the disguises he will employ to get inside our armour.

One of the key ways he does it is by lying to us. But even then he disguises his voice to make it sound like our own. We will talk later about the addiction voice and how to deal with it, but the key is to recognize it for what it is and to shut it off immediately. If I hear my addiction voice and start to argue with it, the voice inside will always have a more convincing argument than I do. It might persuade me that I've had a really tough week, which could be true, but then it will go on to say I will feel so much better if I have a drink or two. And that is a lie.

I have a good friend who recognizes the addiction voice. He tells me that if he listens to it for more than five seconds he is in real trouble. So he addresses the imposter and does something to break the internal dialogue. He might ring a friend, for example, or he might just tell it to get lost.

Once we have got to know ourselves a bit better and understand our vulnerabilities and points of weakness, then we can begin to build up our defences. Recognizing an attack for what it is, is key to being able to select the most appropriate defence response.

We have access to some amazing defence kit: state of the art, proven in battle, and highly effective against attack. If we recognize that we are engaged in a spiritual battle, in our defence armoury we have at our disposal a full set of spiritual weaponry:

> *Therefore put on the full armour of God, so that when the day of evil comes, you may be able to stand your ground, and after you have done everything, to stand. Stand firm then, with the belt of truth buckled around your waist, with the breastplate of righteousness in place, and with your feet fitted with the readiness that comes from the gospel of peace. In addition to all this, take up the shield of faith, with which you can extinguish all the flaming arrows of the evil one. Take the helmet of salvation and the sword of the Spirit, which is the word of God.*

Ephesians 6:13–17 (NIV UK)

It's interesting that the first of these weapons, the belt of truth, means no more denial. Until we are honest with ourselves, we don't find recovery. I make no apology for saying this again; it is a fundamental point. Denial prevents recovery; secrets lead to habits. If you can see truth as a weapon to fight addiction, you will begin to realize just how important it is.

Secondly, we have the breastplate of righteousness. When you fall, get up quickly. Stay in a right relationship with God and with others. If we see righteousness as a gift, we will realize it's something we have to keep asking for. Righteous living will keep you away from dangerous situations.

Thirdly, be willing to do something about your habit, with feet "fitted with the readiness that comes from the gospel of peace".

We then have to learn to trust God when things become hard and "take up the shield of faith, with which you can extinguish all the flaming arrows of the evil one". For "arrows" substitute fear, guilt, pride, and denial.

We must also accept that the battle against addiction has three dimensions: spiritual, emotional, and physical – soul, mind, and body. The mind is a huge battleground. We can win the battle of the mind by recognizing our addiction voice, and not talking to it will be a huge step in winning the war. Through the helmet of salvation we can take captive every thought to make it obedient to Christ.

Finally, we have our greatest weapon against our habits. I love using the sword of the Spirit best of all. I have a thing about swords. The Queen awarded me a Sword of Honour when I graduated top of my intake at Sandhurst. I saluted her with that very sword, and I wore it when I got married. It was the most precious possession I owned. I sold it at the height of my addiction and squandered the cash I got for it in one afternoon. The next morning I called the shop and told them I'd made a terrible mistake and needed it back. But they had already sold it.

The day before Christmas Eve, almost three years later, I had a call from a newspaper to say they had some information about my sword. My heavenly Father has perfect timing. I had just waved my wife and children off. They were spending Christmas Day with

Emma's parents. I wasn't invited and I was feeling a bit sorry for myself.

The sword had been found by an ex-army officer who recognized the significance of a Sword of Honour. He thought it must have been stolen: no one would sell a Sword of Honour. My name is engraved on that Sword, and when he found my name online, he contacted one of the papers that I have shared my story with over the years. They called me. I contacted the shop that was selling it, and bought it there and then. The kind owner of the antique shop arranged for it to be couriered down to me. It arrived on Christmas Eve. I spent most of Christmas looking at it and thanking the Lord for his kindness and grace. I was alone, but very happy.

I would give up that Sword, which after all is only a piece of metal, if I had to choose between it and the sword of the Spirit. The word of God, the Bible, is the most precious treasure I possess now. I pray it always will be. The whole reason I fell into my addiction in the first place was because I stopped reading my Bible, I stopped living in the light, and I stopped listening to God. Sometimes, when we stop listening, he stops talking. My relationship with him just dried up. The only time I really prayed during the three years of my addiction and the weeks leading up to it, as I have mentioned, was to ask God to save my son's life. Guess what: he answered!

Barely a day has passed without me opening my Bible since the day I got down on my knees and asked for forgiveness and healing. Hardly a day goes by when I haven't used the sword of the Spirit. It has become a good habit! I wake up excited about reading; I make a cup of tea and sit in my favourite chair and just soak up the riches of the Bible's wisdom, the joy of hope it brings to my life, and the protection it gives me against my secret habits.

Do you ever have a dream that you went to work or school and realize, too late, that you forgot to get dressed? That's how it feels for me if for some reason I haven't had my biblical fix. I know it's hard, particularly if you are not a morning person. I know for some the evening is when they like to read. Why not dedicate your walk to the station or your place of work to him, or make time in your lunch hour. Whenever you do it, make it part of your daily routine.

Use the Bible when you are under attack, just as Jesus used God's word when he was tempted in the desert (Matthew 4:1–11). Along with prayer, the time you spend listening to him is probably the number one, most effective protection you have against secret habits. You can't cut this corner.

We have looked at a few fundamentals. In the second part of this book we will look at some practical steps we can take to begin to shake off our dark habits and step into the light.

Review

We are engaged in a battle with a spiritual, emotional and physical dimension. Our habits may look deceivingly harmless, or even good. We need to know ourselves better and to recognize the dangers of certain activities in the light of our points of weakness. We need not fear temptation, and we need to employ the spiritual armour of God. Spend time reading the Bible every day.

Exercise

- Resolve to make your quiet time your priority each day. Work out a time of day that suits you and make it your best habit! If you like structure, follow daily notes, such as Nicky Gumbel's online Bible In One Year.

- Write down the times when you feel "under attack", your most vulnerable times (note the place, time, how you are feeling, what you are doing). Look for patterns. These are your triggers.

- At these times of attack, do you notice any trends in what you tell yourself? Begin to recognize this voice as your addiction voice. See the lies for what they are by noting down the words and reading them again the following day.

PART 2

THE PRACTICAL STAGES OF RECOVERY

(STEPS 3 TO 9)

CHAPTER 7

"You Have Control"
(Step 3)

Step 3: "We made a decision to turn our will and our lives over to the care of God."

God, I'm not trying to rule the roost,
I don't want to be king of the mountain.
I haven't meddled where I have no business
or fantasized grandiose plans.

Psalm 131:1 (MSG)

All I ever wanted to do was fly. My own children go through stages of superhero, fireman, postman, and dustman (that last one comes from my autistic son who loves the process of garbage removal). But I only ever wanted to be a pilot. I have to confess to a sense of pride on the day I arrived at the Army Flying School to begin the long and expensive process of becoming a military helicopter pilot. I lost that pride about a week later when I realized I couldn't land. I was fine at flying; I think I was actually quite good at take-off and looping-the-loop, and my "roll-off-the-top" was a thing of beauty. But none of that mattered unless I could land.

I tried and tried, but the harder I tried, the worse I seemed to get. No amount of coaching was helping. My instructor kept telling me, "Let the aeroplane land itself. You're forcing it."

That just made me more frustrated. How can an aeroplane land itself when I control it and it only does what I tell it to? I have to get the flaps at the right angle, I have to juggle the throttles to get the airspeed right, I have to point the nose at the right angle, and then I have to keep playing with the rudder pedals to offset for the crosswind. How can the ****** aeroplane do all that by itself?!

While all the other budding pilots were going solo, every time I attempted to put the aeroplane on the runway, I heard the urgent voice of my instructor through the intercom: "I have control!" That meant he was taking control of the aircraft away from me to avoid an imminent mid-air collision, or a dangerous and embarrassingly heavy landing known as a pancake. My immediate response was to surrender the controls with the words, "You have control!"

They were the last words I ever spoke in the air as a trainee military pilot. I had just avoided another mid-air collision by a matter of a few metres when the officer commanding the Army Flying School called me into his office and bluntly told me I was not cut out to be a pilot and that I would probably kill myself or someone else if I persisted. I was "chopped". With one or two anger issues that I didn't deal too well with at the time, I immediately volunteered for the Royal Artillery, a regiment that specializes in shooting aircraft down.

I don't want to spend too long on the issue of control, because it is tied in to denial (honesty), which we have already looked at, and with pride, which we will look at later. However, if you are holding on to your habit because you don't want to let go, if you are like I was when I said to myself, "I am the one who has got myself into this problem, I am the only one who can get myself out of it," then you may have a few issues with control.

Here are a few clues if you don't already know.

- Do you find it easy to be a passenger, or do you always drive if you have a choice?
- If you are walking, or you are on a long journey that involves directions or map reading, do you like to know where you are and what the next turning is? Do you like to check if someone else is navigating? Or are you always the navigator?

- Do you enjoy being the banker when you play Monopoly?
- Do you like to keep the remote control for the TV near your seat?
- Do you prefer to take the lead if you are in a small group situation? Do you find it hard to let others lead the group discussions? Do you see your role as a facilitator to let others speak, or do you like to try and fix other people's problems for them with your advice?
- If you attend an addiction fellowship, do you share a therapy more often than not?

You get the message. I probably answered yes to most of them!

If you feel the same, then there is a good chance you like being in control. When it comes to recovery, control is not a good thing. Let's face it, while I was in control, my habit just caused destruction. In fact, for many, control is their addiction. It can have catastrophic consequences on relationships. We will only get the help we so desperately need when we realize that we can't land the plane ourselves. That moment when we look up, when we finally relinquish control, is when we discover our God is a far better pilot than we ever could be. He's there waiting for us to hand over control.

In step 3, "We made a decision to turn our will and our lives over to the care of God." When we do this, we need to accept that we are handing him the keys in complete humility. We are asking him to do the driving. You need to say, "You have control." We do this once and for all when we become Christians and ask him into our hearts, but we need to *keep on* handing over control, turning our will (our daily endeavours, our ambitions, our desires, our hopes, and our dreams) to his perfect care. Not to his wrath or judgment, but to his *care*. There will be a much better outcome for our lives if we do this before our habits lead to a mid-air collision. Collisions are messy, destructive, and have long-lasting effects. Believe me. I caused one. Although the crisis has passed, I still deal with the fallout every time I say goodbye to my children at the end of a weekend and drive home alone. I caused pain to the other people I collided with. My actions still cause them pain and will cause them pain in years to come. Please, hand over control before it leads to catastrophe.

As addicts, we need to continually turn our wills and our lives over, on a daily basis. This is especially true if you, like me, like to think you are good at the controls. The reason control is the subject of the first chapter in part two of this book is that handing over control is a deliberate act. Unlike denial, which is a state of mind, handing over control is something we have to *do*. We need to repent of the past and turn our will over to the care of God.

Like the other chapters in this part of the book, you will need to actually do the suggested exercise each time so you can move forward in your recovery. Ideally you should try to do each exercise before you move on to the next chapter. The steps are sequential; they follow an order that needs to be kept to. Each step builds on the recovery from the previous step. The exercise at the end of this chapter continues to deal with the spiritual dimension of your habit.

Accepting that God is the only one who can restore our lives and give us back our freedom is incredibly liberating. It takes the pressure off us without removing the responsibility, because of the way God works. He works in partnership with us. He doesn't impose his will on us. Step three says, "We made the decision to ..." You are not God and you cannot do it on your own, but you do need to make that decision to hand over your will.

When we become Christians by accepting the sovereignty of Christ over our lives, we do it once for all time. However, turning our will and our lives over to his care is something we need to do daily when we pray, asking God to be with us and guide us through the day. You won't be able to get past this step unless you recognize your powerlessness over the addiction or habit. If you can accept that, then you can accept that the solution to the problem probably won't be something you can come up with on your own.

Often, if I need some practical wisdom about a situation, I turn to the book of Proverbs. Here is a gem:

Trust in the Lord with all your heart;
do not depend on your own understanding. Seek his will in all you do,
and he will show you which path to take.

Proverbs 3:5–6

If you have issues with control, it's time to let go. Time to say, "You have control, Lord." When we do this, Jesus tells us what will happen in Matthew 11:28–30. I like *The Message* translation:

"Are you tired? Worn out? Burned out on religion? Come to me. Get away with me and you'll recover your life. I'll show you how to take a real rest. Walk with me and work with me — watch how I do it. Learn the unforced rhythms of grace. I won't lay anything heavy or ill-fitting on you. Keep company with me and you'll learn to live freely and lightly."

There were times when my addiction wore me out. I was exhausted with the lies and the covering up, with the stress of daily life, and living with the knowledge that one day I would be exposed. What a relief it was on the day I realized God still loved me even though I had behaved so badly.

In the next chapter we will look at the first really practical step we can take on our journey of recovery: our moral inventory. It is also one of the hardest.

Review

Submission to God is a choice, a daily act of will. If you think you can fix the problem on your own, think again. Turning our will and our life over to God's care is something we need to do regularly. When we do, we will experience his grace and find freedom. Let go.

Exercise

- On a blank piece of paper, list the different parts of your life. You don't need to put them in any order; just make sure you list them all. For example, you might put your work life, family life, finances, church, hobbies, and key relationships.

- Submit once again to God's will and give him control of every part of your life by praying through each heading.

- Be open to the fact that you might find it easier to give him control in some parts than others. These hard ones are the ones to watch!

- Make a new prayer list and include a note to give him control of your life, including and maybe specifically mentioning, the parts you found the hardest.

- Resolve to pray through your prayer list with God every day.

CHAPTER 8

Moral Inventory and Resentments
(Step 4)

Step 4: "We made a searching and fearless moral inventory of ourselves."

So clean house! Make a clean sweep of malice and pretense, envy and hurtful talk. You've had a taste of God. Now, like infants at the breast, drink deep of God's pure kindness. Then you'll grow up mature and whole in God.

1 Peter 2:1–3 (MSG)

I woke up at 4.30 a.m. in a moment of complete clarity. Something had been bothering me for weeks, and now I knew exactly what I had to do. It was still dark outside. I could hear the rain lashing against my bedroom window, the wind whistling as it gusted between the eaves of the little one-bedroomed barn conversion I now called my home. I fired up my laptop and began to compose the email. The words did not flow. Although I knew what I had to do, actually doing it was much harder. I gave up after the first line and made a cup of tea.

The memory of a phone call from almost twenty years before had woken me. I had taken the call halfway through a six-week live firing exercise on the plains of central Canada. It came as a complete surprise to me. I was a 26-year-old captain serving in an artillery unit that supported the Royal Marines. I had just completed one of the most challenging military selection courses in the world and I was a fully trained military parachutist. I had already served in Northern Ireland during the Troubles and was about to deploy to the war-torn Balkans. I wasn't capable of crying or showing any emotion when I heard the news that my dad had walked out on my mum.

I had always thought my mother and father had an amazing relationship. I never heard them argue. I felt numb at first and then very angry that my dad had just gone and left my mum alone to fend for herself. He'd also walked out on me and all five of my brothers and sisters. Now, on a wet and dark November morning, I realized I had been living with that same anger and resentment for nearly twenty years.

It took me most of the day and many failed attempts before I was even remotely happy with the words of the email. Even then I hesitated to send it. Why was it so hard to forgive, to let go, and to move on? But I knew I had to. I knew my holding on to the resentment was hurting me more than it was hurting my dad.

When I sent it, I felt a huge relief. I wasn't expecting a reply. My forgiveness wasn't conditional. I just wanted my dad to know something I had been unable to tell him ever since he had packed his bag and driven away. My lack of forgiveness meant I hadn't even wanted him to know the truth: that I still loved him and that I missed him, all the time.

So I was surprised when he sent me back a reply that very same day. He told me he loved me too. I read it twice. I couldn't see the words clearly the first time, as my eyes were full of tears of joy. I felt released.

I realized then that by carrying my lack of forgiveness, I had been enslaving myself. Resentment is the result of hardening ourselves to situations, people, or organizations that have hurt or wounded us. When we suppress resentment, the results are anger, frustration, and even depression. There is a quote, the source of which is unclear, although the earliest written reference appears to originate from Alcoholics Anonymous, that holding on to resentment is like drinking poison and waiting for the other person to die.

That afternoon I felt a huge sense of release. While my anger had been directed towards my dad, I had been the one locked up. What I kept locked up internally may have expressed itself externally through my destructive behaviour. I am certain this could be articulated more eloquently by psychologists. I just knew I felt better.

Walking on air

It reminded me a little of what my soldiers and I used to call walking on air. It's the closest I have ever come to flying safely! We often had to cross Dartmoor carrying heavy packs full of equipment, radios and spare batteries, water, rations, and ammunition. The ground underfoot was frequently boggy and uneven. Every few hours we would need to take a break. When we took off our heavy packs and walked without them, just for a few seconds, it felt like we were walking on air, as though gravity didn't exist and we were flying! That's how I felt for the rest of that day, like a heavy weight had been taken off my shoulders. That day I really understood what the theologian Lewis Smedes meant when he said, "To forgive is to set a prisoner free and discover that prisoner is you."

As I begin to understand myself better I see the incredible wisdom in the teaching of Christ when he became a man. He really knew how we function as humans. He knew our frailties and weaknesses, and the practical teaching he left with us is so good for our souls, and also for our minds and our bodies. I was reading the News Review in a popular broadsheet newspaper a few weekends ago. It contained an article about an amazing breakthrough in health. New research has been conducted and it has been discovered that letting go of grudges brings "huge physical and mental benefits". Yes, folks, it's true, forgiveness is good for our health!

In a 2009 study, Dr Robert Enright, a developmental psychologist at the University of Wisconsin-Madison, found that when cardiac patients underwent forgiveness therapy, the blood flow to their hearts improved.[5]

Two thousand years before this research was commissioned, Jesus was giving free health advice. He goes on telling us today through his word.

Although we would all probably accept that letting go of resentments is good for us, it is not easy, as I found when I tried to compose the note to my dad. The hard thing is often to recognize that we hold resentments in the first place, resentments which, like mine, are deeply entrenched and long-standing. Many of them may be justified and arise as a result of the cruelty of others. Sexual, emotional, or physical abuse suffered in childhood is an example. I heard recently that as few as one in eight children who suffer abuse ever report it.

Maybe you were made redundant through no fault of your own. Maybe you or someone you love was involved in an accident that wasn't your or their fault. I'm not saying forgiveness is easy, just that unless we find the courage and grace to let go, we will be suffering the consequences. Just as Jesus showed us how to pray, we need to forgive others as well as receive forgiveness from God. Before we deal with the issue of forgiveness for others, it helps to understand our own faults as well as the resentments we are holding on to so tightly, to understand what we need to be forgiven for as well as our own lack of forgiveness for other people.

Make an inventory

In step 4 we are encouraged to make "a searching and fearless moral inventory of ourselves". This step can take years because we are

---

5   *Telegraph*, 5 September 2015.

probably carrying pain and hurt and all the subsequent resentments without even knowing it. In addition, a full moral inventory is not something we are going to find it particularly comfortable to complete. It will involve looking at our priorities, our integrity, what we think, and what we do.

That's scary however you look at it. You may be thinking, "Hang on, if I go digging up the past, it's going to do more harm than good. I've buried my pain; I don't want to dig it up. It's dealt with; it's in the past. It's not doing any harm." But the problem is that it *is* doing harm; even if it is not doing so now, it will at some stage. This is the key to lasting recovery and a part of your journey that encompasses the spiritual, emotional, and physical dimensions.

Spiritually, we make an inventory and share it with God so that he can mend, heal, and forgive. It may even be that we harbour resentments against God – that must go on the list too. Perhaps we are cross that he hasn't answered a prayer, or hasn't answered in the way we wanted him too. Maybe we are angry because he allowed suffering to happen to others, or to ourselves.

Emotionally, the pain is in your head and it will be affecting the way you see and perceive the world around you. Writing down your list of resentments means the pain they cause can become more than just a set of emotions: they become tangible and not just bottled up; they can be dealt with.

Physically, resentments and pain cause you stress and worry which can lead to depression and other mental illness. You may not be aware of the pain, but until it has been dealt with and released, it is still there. My mother talks about the pain cupboard and how, as we go through life, we put all our hurts, broken dreams, and damaged relationships inside the cupboard until it becomes so full, it just can't take any more. That's what happened to me. Something had to give.

A searching inventory means it is thorough and comprehensive. I met a young chap through The Recovery Course I have been running. We talked about his inventory. He said he had identified

187 resentments and was still working on it. My mother had some resentment against God she didn't even know existed until she went away on a retreat. She was looking for the answer to something, but he didn't tell her what she wanted to hear; instead he showed her that she was holding resentment. She wrote the resentment she had against God on a piece of paper, tied it to a rock, and hurled it into the sea. It was a very physical response to a spiritual blockage, a very human way of dealing with a problem on another dimension.

This is exactly why we need to respond to issues inside us in a tangible way. We must physically write down our inventory, to give life to our "concepts". This means we will be able to find closure to something that has been very real to us, but only real in our heads. There it will remain trapped, until we release it and find we are set free. We need to draw it out into the light and then allow God to take it from us.

The resentments and hurts may remain inside you, dormant and silent, until one day something happens to trigger a memory and they will come back to bite you. They need to be removed.

As a child, I went to the dentist regularly and my teeth had room to grow normally; I never had to wear a brace. When I left home and before I joined the army, I studied physical education at college. I can remember after a long summer at home, I was just getting ready for the new term when my mother said to me, "Justyn, you have such lovely teeth. They are all even and well-spaced." I gave her a flashing smile.

About a month later, I knocked my front teeth out in a clash of heads in a game of hockey. One of them came clean out, but the other one had snapped, leaving the root in my gum.

I pleaded with the dentist not to go through with the gum surgery. I told him there was no pain and you couldn't actually see the root, so what was the need? He was adamant that the root had to come out or it would cause me trouble at some point in the future. I still remember the agony, and to this day I hate visiting the dentist. But the root is gone, and my teeth don't ever bother me.

This step is a bit like root canal surgery. It's painful because we have to confront our weaknesses and our pain. But if we don't do it we will, at some point, suffer the consequences. If we are honest enough to admit we have destructive habits, we are probably already suffering in some way. So your inventory needs to be searching and you need to be fearless about doing it. Fear prevents recovery more than anything else. Fear will stop you from making a searching moral inventory. Fear is an inbuilt human survival instinct. However, unhealthy fear is when we overestimate the danger and underestimate our ability to cope. Take the plunge and you will not regret it. Follow the exercises at the end of this chapter.

There are a few practical things you should do before you start.

Pray first for courage, remembering that with Christ we need fear nothing in this life. Please don't attempt to start your inventory without the protection of prayer. You need to pray for protection and that you will have the courage to overcome your fear. You need to ask the Lord to shine his light into your heart, even the shadowy areas you don't acknowledge from day to day.

And the Holy Spirit helps us in our weakness. For example, we don't know what God wants us to pray for. But the Holy Spirit prays for us with groanings that cannot be expressed in words. And the Father who knows all hearts knows what the Spirit is saying, for the Spirit pleads for us believers in harmony with God's own will.

Romans 8:26–27

In the next part of the book, we will look at fear in more detail, as well as some practical ways to manage it. Please remember you are not alone. When he ascended, Christ left us his helper, the Holy Spirit, who will work with you on this. Remember also that God already knows your heart, so ask him to reveal it to you in line with his will for your life.

It's also really important to remember that this is your inventory. It's not a list of the things other people have done to you, however justified your resentment may be. It is your reaction to the actions of others that is causing the pain now. You can't change what happened, but you can choose to let go of the resentment and hurt you feel. Don't list the faults of others; list your own feelings. You might think it's not your fault that you have become reliant on habits that you use as a defence against the pain others have inflicted on you. You can't change their actions. But you can choose not to carry round the hurt, because the pain and the resentment are causing you to use. Let them go. They are destructive and superfluous, and they stop you feeling the love your Father has for you.

I also strongly recommend that before you start your inventory, you spend some time reminding yourself of some of the good things you have done in your life. The purpose of this inventory is not to conduct a character assassination on yourself or to lower your self-esteem any further. The purpose is to set you free of anything that is pulling you down and back over your start line. In his book *Breathing Underwater*, Richard Rohr gives a very good reason for not needing to be apprehensive about your inventory:

> *God uses our sins in our own favour! God brings us – through failure – from unconsciousness to ever-deeper consciousness and conscience. How could that not be good news for just about everybody?*[6]

It's also a step which is very grounded biblically:

> *Investigate my life, O God,*
> *find out everything about me;*
> *Cross-examine me and test me,*
> *get a clear picture of what I'm about;*
> *See for yourself whether I've done anything wrong –*
> *then guide me on the road to eternal life.*

Psalm 139:23–24 (MSG)

---

6   Richard Rohr, *Breathing Underwater* (1989).

Find a quiet moment, make yourself a hot drink, get a pen and paper or your electronic device of choice, settle down, and do this chapter's exercises. These are exercises you need to do before going any further. Remember, it's not a list of the things people have done to you, nor is it a list of your wrongs; it's just a list of the resentments you hold. It will probably surprise you. It certainly surprised me when I did it.

By the way, you can't do this in your head. The act of writing it down or typing it out is important to the process. Don't expect to do it in one go, either. It may take time. If you are anything like me, your list will frequently have new things added, and in time you can take things off. Keep your inventory somewhere safe. Don't share it with anyone just yet. We will talk about what to do with it in the next chapter. Don't expect perfection either; just make a start. One day at a time.

Review

Resentments harm you. Carrying unresolved conflict and pain harms you. If you prayerfully write a detailed moral inventory it will allow you to begin to recognize the resentment and rubbish you have been carrying around with you. You need to recognize that it will be painful, and pray for the courage to overcome your fear.

Exercise

- Pray for wisdom, enlightenment, and courage before you start.

- Write a brief summary of four good things you have done in your life, things you look back on with joy.

- Draw a table with three columns. Give the first column the heading "Who", the next "Why", and the third "How".

- Under the heading "Who", make a note of all the people, organizations, or establishments against whom you are holding a grudge.

- Under the "Why" heading, for each person you noted in the previous column, make a note of what happened that led to your grudge.

- Under the final heading, "How", make a note of how the event affected you personally, how it made you feel at the time, and how it still makes you feel. Write down who was at fault.

CHAPTER 9

Confession and Removal
(Steps 5 to 7)

Step 5: "We admitted to God, to ourselves, and to another human being the exact nature of our wrongs."

Step 6: "We were entirely ready to have God remove all these defects of character."

Step 7: "We humbly asked God to remove our shortcomings."

Make allowance for each other's faults, and forgive anyone who offends you. Remember, the Lord forgave you, so you must forgive others.

Colossians 3:13

But if we confess our sins to him, he is faithful and just to forgive us our sins and to cleanse us from all wickedness.

1 John 1:9

Clearing out the garage

I always wanted a workshop. In my mind, my workshop would have all the latest power tools to make every job easy. I could be creative there, make shelves that would impress my wife. Every tool would have its place, neatly stored away so I would always know where it was in the event of an emergency. In my imagination, I even painted a silhouette of each tool by its hook, so I could see if one was missing.

When I knew Emma was coming back, I found a house that was big enough for us all to live in. One of the reasons I chose to move into that particular house was that it had a large garage with a light and power sockets. It would make the perfect workshop. I never quite managed to create that workshop, and before I had the chance, Emma had moved on.

Do you have a dumping ground, a space where you put the things that you just can't find a proper place for? The toys your children have grown out of but you can't bring yourself to throw away or take to the charity shop. Or that vacuum cleaner you replaced because it blew out more dust that it sucked up, but you just cannot bring yourself to throw it away because you think you might need it one day.

I had a space like that. The garage that I had dreamed of turning into a workshop became my dumping ground. It was packed so full, I was afraid to open the door in case everything fell out. I kept all my old tools there, but they were not neatly stored. I could never find that one tool I really needed without hunting around and creating even more disorder.

The roof leaked when it rained and the tools I stored there became useless, and the blades were blunt. Even the nails and screws I once kept neatly sorted in their own individual compartments, according to size, became jumbled together in a damp, rusted mess at the bottom of my toolbox. I knew I needed a good weekend to clear up and make a couple of trips to the local tip. And yet it was a job I kept putting off. I was scared of finding things that would cause me too much pain to touch, objects that would remind me of the past. Things like Oscar's cot, the musical mobile we used to turn on in the middle of the night with a tune that always sent him to sleep, his first bike with stabilizers. I really wanted it to be a workshop, but instead the garage was full of the junk and clutter we all seem to collect as we go through life.

Things didn't work out the way I had planned. I put off clearing out the garage until the last possible moment. I don't think I would ever have got round to it if events hadn't unfolded in the way they had over the summer.

We had all been on our family holiday to Devon together: Emma, me, and the boys. It was a lovely holiday, and I had no inkling of what was to follow. I came home while she went to stay with her parents. After a few weeks she sent me a text to say she wasn't coming back. The trust I had betrayed three years before had never fully returned. She never quite saw me in the same way again after she found out I had a secret gambling habit. Although she knew I had turned my back on my destructive addiction and she could see I had become a new person, that new person wasn't the one she had married. We had tried to rebuild our marriage, to fall in love all over again. And while I found that easy to do, I knew she was finding it harder, so I put up barriers to protect myself. I didn't show her the practical love I felt so deeply.

When the shock wore off and I realized she wasn't coming back, I packed up the house. It was time to move on and find a new home. Clearing the garage was the last job before I handed back the keys to what had been our family home. It has been a place of hope and new beginnings, but ultimately it became a place where we had failed to rebuild our relationship.

Clearing the garage was hard work, physically and emotionally. I had to confront a past I thought I had buried as I sorted through the things that held so many memories. It was almost brutal. And the tears began to fall. At first they were tears of self-pity, loss, and rejection. I didn't like throwing out the familiar, but quite useless, things I found. They felt like old friends. But then something shifted inside me. As the pile for the tip grew, the garage became emptier, and the clear space began to hold hope. It took me three trips to the tip, and every time I threw something into the huge containers I felt a release. I had been holding on to my past so tightly, holding on to the clutter and junk, holding on to the dream of a future I wanted in the way I wanted it.

Although I had emptied out the garage, it wasn't yet clean. It had taken me most of the day, and now it was getting dark the corners of the garage were concealed by shadows. When I turned on the light I could see the floor was coated in dust. One last sweep through and the job was done. The garage was now a useful space again, not just a place to dump clutter. It would become a great workshop for someone else.

As we allow God to shine his light inside us, it reveals all the pain, resentment, rejection, and lack of forgiveness we hold on to. But as we store up more and more pain, we have less room for him. It can be painful and it might take time, but as we hand it all back to him and let it go, unpack it and take it to the tip, throw it over our start line, we make more room for Christ. He has more room to fill us up with his love, his presence, his Holy Spirit, and we can experience more intimacy, more love, more joy, more peace, patience, kindness, and self-control. As we become closer to him, more intimate with him, we become more like him, and the reasons we had for our destructive behaviour cease to have their power. We are no longer "white knuckling" our recovery by our own willpower; we are truly set free. We are on the long-term road to recovery, freedom, and true happiness; something we thought we could find by indulging our own pleasure. We find, instead, that we are truly satisfied, not just temporarily distracted, because we have a fountain of life-giving water that will truly sustain us and meet our every need. That is true freedom.

He also has a new set of tools for us. It's time to throw out those rusty nails and the blunt saw that wouldn't cut through balsa wood. Christ has a new set for us, shining and sharp. He wants us to make a carpenter's workshop in our lives for him, so he can come in and use the tools he has given us to make beautiful things. It's time to tidy up your garage, to go back to your start line and hand your shortcomings to Christ.

If I were a psychoanalyst, I would say that if our inner being is cluttered and disorganized, packed full of junk or painful memories, then it might lead to compulsive external behaviour patterns that seek to create order in the physical world around us. We try to impose ourselves on the outside by indulging in damaging behaviour patterns where we seek to satisfy our cravings or numb our emotions and true needs. This behaviour is harmful to ourselves and the ones we love. We don't respect or value ourselves as we should. If we don't feel loved, we find it hard to love ourselves the way we should. And yet, if we could only glimpse a fraction of the love that our Creator has for us, we would feel secure, confident, and totally loved. You are loved by God in a way you can't even comprehend. That realization was for me such a source of reassurance at a time when my marriage was falling apart and someone I loved did not love me in the same way.

We are his temple, his dwelling place. We should respect that. In spite of all our perceived imperfections, still he loves us. We are also made by him. Who are we to criticize his creation? This verse is underlined in my Bible in three different colours, and it really sums up what we need to do to allow Christ to come and heal us from the inside:

But now is the time to get rid of anger, rage, malicious behavior, slander, and dirty language. Don't lie to each other, for you have stripped off your old sinful nature and all its wicked deeds. Put on your new nature, and be renewed as you learn to know your Creator and become like him.

Colossians 3:8–10

Are you thinking "I wish he would stop talking in metaphors and explain how I can take my inventory to the tip"? That's the easy bit. I had to go to the tip myself and clear out my physical junk. When we ask God to remove our resentments, he comes round with a big removal van and does it for us. Some things we might be able to hand over quickly. Others we may be holding on to a bit too tightly, and they might take longer to give away.

Writing your inventory was the hard part, but it will help you to let go. You need to take your inventory to the place I took my mask wardrobe. Take it all to the foot of the cross, and there you need to go through each line and admit where you have been wrong. In humility, not self-pity, you need to repent and say sorry to God and to ask him to take the resentments on your list away.

By physically writing the inventory and by taking it to the foot of the cross, you will already have admitted these things to yourself. And they exist, they can be removed. It's a bit like when you pack your things into storage boxes before the removal company comes to take them away.

Now take the list and find someone you trust. If you can go through it with them too, it will become so much more meaningful, although it might be harder. This will also act to re-establish relationships and your sense of community, and reduce the isolation you felt when you started hiding your habits.

When we confess our sins, we take down the barriers we erected and now we can receive forgiveness. More practical wisdom from Proverbs 28:13: "You can't whitewash your sins and get by with it; you find mercy by admitting and leaving them" (MSG).

Eugene Peterson, in *The Message* translation of Romans 8, talks about our freedom to no longer "live under a continuous, low-lying black cloud" and how the "Spirit of life in Christ, like a strong wind, has magnificently cleared the air" (verses 1–2).

In completing our "searching and fearless" moral inventory (step 4), we will have come to realize we have faults, shortcomings, and sin. Dumping them at the tip means we need to confess them before God and ask for his forgiveness, and then ask him to take them away.

In step 7 we "humbly asked God to remove our shortcomings". He can and will accept our baggage. The skip is big enough for everything, so don't hold on to anything. Just let it go.

In the next chapter we will look at one of the most satisfying and rewarding parts of our recovery journey: making amends. So far our journey has been introverted, looking at ourselves, but now we can start to look out through the windows and begin to restore our relationships with others.

Review

We need to make room for Christ by clearing out the clutter. When we confess our faults to God, we cut the ties that hold us down and we are set free to soar by the gift of his grace and the certain knowledge of his love for us. When we confess our faults to another person, we re-establish a sense of community and step out of the shadow of isolation and into the light of accountability.

Exercise

- Spend time in confession before God and go through your inventory, line by line, asking for forgiveness.
- Accept God's forgiveness and let go of feelings of guilt and shame.
- Take the inventory and talk it through with someone you trust.

CHAPTER 10

Making Amends
(Steps 8 and 9)

Step 8: "We made a list of all persons we had harmed, and became willing to make amends to them all."

Step 9: "We made direct amends to such people wherever possible, except where to do so would injure them or others."

"Here is a simple rule of thumb for behaviour: Ask yourself what you want people to do for you; then grab the initiative and do it for them! ... I tell you, love your enemies. Help and give without expecting a return. You'll never – I promise – regret it ... Be easy on people; you'll find life a lot easier. Give away your life; you'll find life given back, but not merely given back – given back with bonus and blessing. Giving, not getting, is the way."

Luke 6:31–38 (MSG)

Sorry is the hardest word

Six months free of gambling and I was going through my spiritual steps. I felt forgiven and had even begun to forgive myself. So far all the steps had been about me. I was making my step 8 list of all the people I had harmed, and I was willing to make amends to them all. I wanted to get on with step 9 where I would actually make the amends. I was looking forward to it. It was going to be a huge weight off my shoulders. I don't think I really grasped the fact that steps 8 and 9 were more about other people than about myself.

Emma and I were making plans to get back together. Her family had been really hurt by my actions. Emma had three brothers; she was the only daughter and the youngest child. Her family felt protective, of course they did. I could accept that; I totally understood that. I wanted to make everything right. At the very top of my inventory of people I had hurt was Emma's father.

"I can't even talk about you round the meal table at home. I just think it would break his heart if I told him I was moving south to get back with you." It was late. The boys were fast asleep. Emma and I were talking on the phone. It was her father she was most concerned about too.

"What can I do to make it better, Emma? How can I show him I've changed?" I asked.

"I think a lot of it has to do with money. He wants to know I will be financially secure again. Maybe you could send him a cheque and just write a letter, apologizing."

"OK," I said. "I'll do it."

I knew my father-in-law was a traditionalist. So the next day I wrote a long letter in my own hand. I apologized for causing pain and accepted full responsibility. I told him I would really like another chance to look after his daughter. I wrote a cheque for an amount I could afford. Then I ripped up the cheque and wrote a new one for even more.

I posted the letter and felt much better. A couple of days later, I was at home at my mother's house when the post was delivered. I met the postman at the door. None of the letters was for me. I realized I was waiting for a reply from Emma's father to say he was willing to forgive me.

As the days passed, I began to feel more and more frustrated. *Why hasn't he written?* I checked with my bank. The cheque had been cashed.

I called Emma. "Has he said anything about me? Has he mentioned my letter?"

"No. Are you sure it arrived?" she asked.

As the weeks passed, I realized I was expecting him to forgive me. What I felt when he didn't reply was something like traffic rage. You know what I mean: when you courteously give up your right of way to let another car through and they ignore you. If they don't even acknowledge your kindness, it makes you mad. My desire to make amends came with conditions. I was doing it to reconcile a situation and be welcomed back into Emma's family. I should have simply said sorry and not expected any response. I should have just taken care of my side of the street and realized I could do nothing more. If my father-in-law chose not to forgive me, then that was between him and God. It was nothing to do with me.

I should have listened to Jesus when he said, "I tell you, love your enemies. Help and give without expecting a return. You'll never – I promise – regret it. Live out this God-created identity the way our Father lives toward us, generously and graciously, even when we're at our worst. Our Father is kind; you be kind" (Luke 6:35, MSG).

I gave, but I expected a return. I was setting myself up for disappointment. I wasn't truly willing to say sorry; my apology had strings: "You forgive me so I can carry on where I left off."

We need to be willing to make amends to everyone we have hurt, but it takes wisdom to know when and how to make amends. Step 9 says, "We made direct amends to such people wherever possible, except where to do so would injure them or others."

I hadn't considered that perhaps my apology was coming too soon and that it would make him more angry than merciful. We can be willing to make amends, but the wisest course of action may sometimes be to do nothing. We have to remember that when we ask for forgiveness, we give the other person the chance to be free. This is something we actually do for others. Addiction is all about the individual, and sometimes we can see our recovery as an equally selfish process. By seeking to make amends, we give other people the chance to recover. So the way we seek to make amends shouldn't cause them more injury. We have to be careful not to cause them embarrassment, or to stir up more resentment. Addiction is self-indulgent; it's downright selfish. In seeking to make amends, we need to be sensitive and prayerful before we jump in. Paul gives the following advice in his letter to the Philippians:

> *Don't be selfish; don't try to impress others. Be humble, thinking of others as better than yourselves. Don't look out for your own interests, but take an interest in others too.*
>
> **Philippians 2:3–4**

We have to accept that there may be a right and a wrong time to make amends, and that making amends is not just about getting rid of your guilt; it's about allowing others to forgive you.

It may be that the people we have hurt have passed away. We need to accept that it won't always be possible to ask for forgiveness. But that doesn't mean we should still carry guilt if we have repented before God.

The way we do it is very important. A face-to-face meeting may be right in some situations; a simple "sorry" note may be more appropriate in others, or even a carefully chosen gift. Don't rush this step; take your time and do it right – and remember, this is more about the other person than you.

In *The Big Book of AA*, Bill Wilson explains the benefits for us of making amends:

> *If we are painstaking about this phase of our development we will be amazed before we are halfway through. We are going to know a new freedom and a new happiness. We will not regret the past nor wish to shut the door on it. We will comprehend the word serenity and we will know peace. No matter how far down the scale we have gone, we will see how our experience can benefit others.*[7]

---

7   Bill Wilson, *The Big Book of AA* (1939).

He goes even further when he says that feelings of uselessness and self-pity will disappear, and we will lose interest in selfish things and gain an interest in others. We will stop self-seeking, as our whole attitude to life begins to change. He says the fears we hold on to – fear of people and financial insecurity – will leave us. We will know "how to handle situations that used to baffle us. We will suddenly realize that God is doing for us what we could not do for ourselves."

Making amends lifts our self-esteem while restoring the relationships of our support network, the people we love and need in our life.

If you have been following the exercises and completing these steps, you are a long way into your journey. In fact, I would say you are through the shipping lane and the coast of France is now in sight. But watch out. There is still a long way to go. In the next part we take a look at the ways we can prevent relapse and maintain our recovery.

Review

Making amends seeks to restore broken relationships. We can only offer to those we have hurt the opportunity for reconciliation. This is about their feelings as well as ours. Past hurts affect our future. Peace comes from reconciliation, but it's not about their response; it's about taking responsibility to do the right thing.

Exercise

- Pray for wisdom and sensitivity. Pray that the Holy Spirit will shine light on the hurt you have caused to others.

- Draw a table with three columns. Give the first column the heading "Whom did I hurt or harm?" The next, "How did I hurt or harm them?" The third, "How can I make amends?"

- Under the heading "Whom did I hurt or harm?", make a note of all the people you have hurt through your habit, or even just in the course of your life.

- Under the "How did I harm them?" heading, for each person you noted in the previous column, make a note of what you did to cause their hurt.

- Under the final heading, "How can I make amends?", begin to think about ways you might apologize or make it up to them. Some of these actions you will think of immediately, others may take longer, and some you may feel would cause more harm than good if you were to try. This column will take longer. You need to pray through each situation and seek advice from others before you take action.

- Follow up the actions you have written in the final column, make amends, and experience the relief and joy that comes with it.

PART 3

PREVENTING RELAPSE
(STEPS 10 TO 12)

CHAPTER 11

The Maintenance Steps
(Steps 10 and 11)

Step 10: "We continued to take personal inventory and when we were wrong promptly admitted it."

Step 11: "We sought through prayer and meditation to improve our conscious contact with God, praying only for knowledge of his will for us and the power to carry it out."

Be alert and of sober mind. Your enemy the devil prowls around like a roaring lion looking for someone to devour.

1 Peter 5:8 (NIV UK)

"Anyone who listens to my teaching and follows it is wise, like a person who builds a house on solid rock. Though the rain comes in torrents and the floodwaters rise and the winds beat against that house, it won't collapse because it's built on bedrock. But anyone who hears my teaching and doesn't obey it is foolish, like a person who builds a house on sand. When the rains and floods come and the winds beat against that house, it will collapse with a mighty crash."

Matthew 7:24–27

If you think you are standing strong, be careful not to fall. The temptations in your life are no different from what others experience. And God is faithful. He will not allow the temptation to be more

*than you can stand. When you are tempted, he will show you a way
out so that you can endure.*

1 Corinthians 10:12–13

Taking stock

At the start of the third part to this book, let's take a look at the
journey so far. If you have followed the exercises at the end of each
chapter, you will have taken some massive steps forward in your
recovery. I still actively work on steps 10, 11 and 12, known as the
maintenance steps, but from time to time I also need to go back
and add a resentment or a person to my lists from steps 4 and 8. It
could be an entirely new resentment or person I have hurt, or it may
be an old one the Holy Spirit reveals to me.

I can never take my recovery for granted. Although I am certain
that God has healed me, I still take life one day at a time. I know
I can't have even one bet now without the risk of my life crashing
down. That means I am taking care of step 1: I am not denying the
fact that I can never go back to gambling on an occasional basis. I
am a gambling addict. Through God's gift of grace, I just choose
the freedom of not betting.

So let's look back at what we have achieved, and I will look back
with you at my own journey. Firstly, in steps 1, 2 and 3, we faced up
to our problem, honestly admitting we needed help. We then put
our lives into the care of God.

In steps 4 to 7 we took a good look at our lives and then confessed
and shared our faults. We gave God permission to reorder our lives
and asked him to help turn us into the people we long to be: free.

In steps 8 and 9 we stopped looking inwardly at ourselves and
started to restore our relationships with others by listing those we
had harmed and making amends where appropriate.

That's quite a journey, and you really should feel a sense of
achievement. But it is also a dangerous time.

In the Channel after ten hours at sea, I saw the French coast. I became complacent. I thought I had made it. All through the day I had concentrated on swimming close to my pilot boat. But now, with land in sight, I drifted away from my boat, taken by a gentle but strengthening tide. I thought I was heading directly for land. And then the storm hit.

So many times I congratulate a friend or a guest on The Recovery Course for being free from their habit for major landmarks like six weeks, six months, a whole year or more. Then, just a few weeks later, I see them looking worse than ever. They have relapsed. They are very upset and fearful, full of self-loathing because they really thought they had beaten their habit. They feel like they are worse off than they had been before.

After a year of not using, we are in pretty good shape. We probably feel healthier and happier; maybe our lives are better organized. Our relationships and friendships are in order and our finances may be healthier.

This is when we are most vulnerable to relapse. It is then, when the misery of our old habit is forgotten, that we are hit by a storm. Something happens. It could be an argument, an illness, an unexpected redundancy, or even a success or happy moment. It is then that, without even thinking, we go back to our old ways. Mostly we relapse because we forget step 1: subconsciously we tell ourselves, "I am mended; I have recovered; I'm not an addict any more, so one drink won't hurt. One bet will be fine. I'll just stop; I know how to now." I am working through these steps with you, and step 1 is one of the steps on which I have to keep working.

This chapter looks at the ways we can protect the position we are in. I call it protecting our spiritual health, because that's what it is. If we have completed steps 1 to 9 we are in a good place spiritually. We will be enjoying a certain intimacy with God, free from our habits and, if not completely in the light, we can see the light at the end of the tunnel. This is the time we need to be on our guard. The last three steps are all about maintaining our spiritual health and preventing the slips and relapses that threaten to drag us back over our start lines.

This is important. If you do have a slip, don't give up and let it turn into a full-blown prolonged relapse. Imagine the journey from your house to the nearest train station. When you started your recovery journey, you got on your bike and you started cycling to the station. For some of you the distance is a long one and you have many miles to cover; for others, it is shorter. When you slip up and fall off your bike, what do you do? One thing you never do is pick up your bike and carry it home, then start the journey all over again. You just get back on and keep pedalling. Recovery is the same. None of the work you have done so far is wasted. You never need to go back to your start line except to dump stuff that hinders.

The pretender will feed you every lie in the book. He'll say things like, "You are useless, you can't do it." "You really are beyond help." "Well, that's blown it. You may as well just give in and keep using."

Please don't give up. Just get back on the bike. Just keep taking another stroke. Your spiritual health is so very precious and at first it will be a bit fragile. You need to protect it, and here's how.

Running repairs

If we have followed the steps so far, our lives will be on a much firmer foundation than they were. Our roots will go down deeper into the soil. We don't need to take any drastic action. The rebuilding work is over; the builders have gone and have taken their scaffolding with them. We just need to stay on top of our house-cleaning and garden maintenance. We need to do our running repairs.

Some of us are night owls and some are early birds. I definitely fall into the latter category. I am at my best in the morning. After 9 p.m. I start to go downhill rapidly. I could happily be tucked up in bed at 8 p.m. with a good book and still only manage two pages before falling asleep. I was probably conditioned to be that way from my childhood when I woke most mornings before 6 a.m. to do an hour of swimming training before school. My time in the army did nothing to change my body clock.

If I go to bed struggling with an issue or a problem, I will often wake up with a possible solution. It will be the very first thought that comes into my head. However, if my head is clogged up with guilt or unresolved conflict, I lose my creativity and I damage my spiritual health.

I like to try to give God my best time, my creative time, when I am most alert. That's why I like to wake early, make a pot of tea, and open up my Bible. As I listen to God's word I see many things I need to do. I might feel the need to send someone an email, to give them a word of encouragement or just to say sorry. I can be thick-skinned sometimes, and it's in the morning that I often realize I have been heavy-handed in a conversation or a situation that needed more tact and sensitivity. I am sometimes asked by friends why I ignored them. It's usually because I haven't seen them. I don't multitask very well, so the likelihood is I was thinking about something! The time I spend in God's presence is often the time when I will actually do steps 8 and 9. I will realize I have upset someone and I will instinctively know how to make amends. For all of you who have received a text from me at 5 a.m., I am sorry!

This is the time when I connect best with my Father, and one of the main reasons why my addiction, my habit, was so destructive. It acted like a barrier, a black cloud between me and God. My time around sleep, last thing at night or the first thing in the morning, was when I had to face up to what I had done that day, or the night before. I think it is also one of the reasons why people feel the need to anaesthetize with too much alcohol, so they can avoid the pain of reality at night. Waking with a hangover, or with the knowledge that the day before you gambled away the money you needed to pay the rent, a fuel bill, your train ticket, or the weekly groceries, is a painful thing to do.

Proverbs 23 points out the futility of this cycle:

Who has anguish? Who has sorrow?
Who is always fighting? Who is always complaining?
Who has unnecessary bruises? Who has bloodshot eyes?
It is one who spends long hours in the taverns,
trying out new drinks.
Don't gaze at the wine, seeing how red it is,
how it sparkles in the cup, how smoothly it goes down.
For in the end it bites like a poisonous snake;
it stings like a viper.

Proverbs 23:29–30

The Bible is packed full of wonderful, practical advice and wisdom.

The relationship we have with ourselves is so important. To gauge the health of that relationship, spend time alone, without any sound. Is the thought of that a comfortable one or one that feels a bit scary? The Bible tells us that to improve the way we see ourselves and not rely on how we think people see us, we must "learn to appreciate and give dignity to your body" (1 Thessalonians 4:4, MSG).

If we have followed the journey of this book so far and completed the exercises at the end of each chapter, we will have begun to feel free from the cycle of addiction. We may not necessarily feel fixed, but we should be beginning to feel hope and have dealt with some of the issues or pain that was causing our habit, and begun to experience what freedom feels like. But how can we sustain that; how can we move on from a brief respite to lasting recovery? We may be in a good place now, but we can still be so easily tripped up. How can we really experience freedom?

Steps 10 and 11 point the way. As I have mentioned, they have been described as the maintenance steps, and step 11 has been called the relapse buster! I love that because it feels like what we are doing has power. It does, but the power isn't our own.

The first of these two steps, step 10, is something I would like to be able to do as I drift off to sleep, but generally I find myself doing it in the mornings as I spend time reading my Bible. It says, "We continued to take personal inventory and when we were wrong promptly admitted it."

If you completed the step 4 exercise at the end of chapter 8, you will have a moral inventory. As you continued to read this book and complete the exercises, you will have known what to do about the issues on your inventory. However, we don't suddenly become perfect. We might experience new issues, new resentments, and new conflicts. Continuing to take personal inventory simply means we need to take a look at our lives on a daily basis and think about what we have said or done, or sometimes not said or not done. We need to accept that our action or lack of action can and does cause others pain. Where we were wrong, we need to say sorry. It's as simple as that. The idea is that we avoid conflict, stress, and the build-up of resentments before they can take hold and drag us back over our start lines.

I wish I had the discipline to do this every night, but I am so ready for sleep I don't really manage it. I am more aware of my failures and the things I have done wrong as I wake up and take my personal inventory before God in the morning. The Bible says, "And 'don't sin by letting anger control you.' Don't let the sun go down while you are still angry, for anger gives a foothold to the devil" (Ephesians 4:26–27). I guess I am better at not letting the sun rise before I deal with the issue.

Jesus, while teaching about anger said, "So if you are presenting a sacrifice at the altar in the Temple and you suddenly remember that someone has something against you, leave your sacrifice there at the altar. Go and be reconciled to that person. Then come and offer your sacrifice to God" (Matthew 5:23–24).

In other words, none of us should be worshipping at church if we are holding any form or grudge, resentment, or lack of forgiveness. That's fairly radical to me, but totally supports our life if we want to avoid relapse.

Relapse is a word used frequently in recovery. It seems to be a more serious version of a "slip", where we may go back to our habit once, but we realize why we did it and it doesn't happen again. I would probably accept that a relapse is a more serious situation, where we have turned our back on our recovery and indulged our habit multiple times or binged.

Relapse is not something that just happens. If we engage with our addiction voice in conversation, that's probably when the relapse happens, because our addiction voice will be so plausible. It will try to take us right back to the beginning, to denial. It might say: "Go on, reward yourself, you've done so well." Or, "You have control now; you're not an addict any more. You can have just one drink. Then you can stop." I have dedicated a whole chapter (chapter 13) to practical ways of dealing with the addiction voice.

The tiger cub you locked up in a cage went to sleep when you stopped using. If you let it out now, you will discover it is no longer a cub; it kept on growing and is now a fully grown tiger waiting to rip you apart. If you do have a slip or a relapse, don't beat yourself up. Negativity will pull you back over your start line and drag you back into your cycle of destruction. Just get back up, dust yourself down, and keep taking the next stroke. Please don't try to hide it. You should by now have a small network of people who support you. If you cover up, you are being dishonest with yourself and those around you. Dishonesty is denial, and if you pretend nothing has happened you've just landed on the head of the longest snake on the game board. It will take you right back to step one. Honesty is not optional in recovery. I found out the hardest way of all, so please take my advice.

By continuing to get to know yourself, by understanding when you have behaved badly and doing something about it, by saying sorry (to the person you hurt and/or to God), you set yourself free to keep going. You avoid the stress and conflict that cause us to reach for our medicine of choice.

After Paul tells the Ephesians not to let the sun go down while they are still angry, he urges them to:

Get rid of all bitterness, rage, anger, harsh words, and slander, as well as all types of evil behavior. Instead be kind to each other, tenderhearted, forgiving one another, just as God through Christ has forgiven you.

Ephesians 4:31–32

If those involved in recovery accept that step 10 is best done at the end of the day, they probably would agree that the next step, the second of the relapse preventers, is a great way to start the day. Step 11 says, "We sought through prayer and meditation to improve our conscious contact with God, praying only for knowledge of his will for us and the power to carry it out."

We shouldn't just see prayer as our "morning list", where we run through our prayer requests. At the end of chapter 7, one of the exercises was to write out a new prayer list. Writing a new prayer list is important from time to time. Our needs and requests might change; some of our prayers may have been answered or our situation changed. The intimacy of prayer suggests a constant dialogue between us and our Maker, as we remember always to thank him (1 Thessalonians 5:18). Although the structure of prayer notes can be helpful, prayer should be spontaneous, not scripted, just like our conversations with those we love. Sometimes we are only able to express our hearts through "groanings" (Romans 8:26).

How can we have a relationship with someone if we don't take the time to listen to what they say and to speak to them? I love meeting older couples who have been happily married for many years. Have you seen the way they seem so alike? Their routines are so similar, their mannerisms, their humour, and their interests. The more time we spend with God, listening to him through the Bible and talking to him in prayer, the more we will become like Christ. Sometimes I make the mistake of seeing my prayer time as just a list of needs I run through. It's then that I try to remind myself of the privilege we have through Christ of being able to talk directly to the Creator of the universe. This helps me to add in the "thank yous" and the words of love and affection, as well as the requests.

Psalm 119 is the longest psalm, with 176 verses. It's a beautiful psalm, all about God's word. In verse 29 there is a prayer we would all do well to memorize: "Keep me from lying to myself; give me the privilege of knowing your instructions."

That verse is a perfect summary of how we can achieve lasting recovery.

Review

We need to protect our spiritual health. Each day we need to take time to think about the good things and the bad things we have done. When we have hurt others, we need to take responsibility and apologize. Through prayer, we need to improve our spiritual health and our relationship with God, and ask him to reveal his will and to give us the strength to carry it out.

Exercise

- Set a little time aside at the end of each day, or first thing in the morning, to go through the day, or the previous day, in your mind. Some may prefer to use a notebook and jot down the key events. If so, make a note of the good things you did.

- Accept also that you may have behaved badly in certain situations. Deal with these by making amends, or saying sorry as soon as you can. If it is a particularly significant conflict that can't be resolved simply, it may need to go on to your step 8 list (see the exercise at the end of chapter 10).

- Review your prayer list. Make sure it has space to thank God and to express your love for him. It should also have room to request knowledge of his will for you and the strength to carry it out.

CHAPTER 12

Helping Others
(Step 12)

Step 12: "Having had a spiritual awakening as the result of these steps, we tried to carry this message to those still in active addiction, and to practice these principles in all our affairs."

So let's do it — full of belief, confident that we're presentable inside and out. Let's keep a firm grip on the promises that keep us going. He always keeps his word. Let's see how inventive we can be in encouraging love and helping out, not avoiding worshiping together as some do but spurring each other on, especially as we see the big Day approaching.

Hebrews 10:24 (MSG)

As an author, I have the privilege of receiving messages from people who have read my book *Tails I Lose*. My editorial team should take all the credit for suggesting the last page of that book be a "Contact the author" page. The two most frequently asked questions, other than "Help?" are, "Should I tell my husband or wife?" and, "How can I get involved in helping others?"

It is one of the human traits that we are blessed with, that when we have been through a tough experience, we want to help others. When it comes to addiction, the process of helping others helps to sustain and solidify our own recovery. There is something very healing about being a healer. I have also come to realize that, although there are some brilliant and inspiring trained counsellors, the very best people to help recovering addicts are other recovering addicts.

It is a very human response to look for reason and meaning after we have recovered from a shock or a traumatic experience. For me, following the twelve steps transformed me from someone who dared not look back on the horror of my three-year addiction to someone who was willing to go back there and find the healing I needed, by putting it to rest and dealing with the pain. I still suffer the consequences of my actions even now, but I know how to deal with the pain, and I welcome the forgiveness I have experienced through God's grace.

There is something very lovely about the way God uses our weaknesses and turns them into strengths, into tools he can use for his glory. I love to see the way God uses the broken, the humble, and the damaged. It's why we never need to give up on life. We can counter the deceiver's lies by saying, "Even though I made a mess of things, this experience is not wasted if I let God use it for his glory." Paul sums it up when he says, "And we know that God causes everything to work together for those who love God and are called according to his purpose for them" (Romans 8:28).

And again in his second letter to the Corinthians: " 'My grace is all you need. My power works best in weakness.' So now I am glad to boast about my weaknesses, so that the power of Christ can work through me" (2 Corinthians 12:9). In the very next verse, Paul even makes the point that when he is weak, then he is strong. This is exactly why we, as recovering addicts, can be so powerful for Christ. We know we have sinned and yet, through Christ, we have been set free. We have experienced his grace, and we have hope because we have suffered slavery but also experienced the exquisite taste of freedom.

Addiction is not well understood by those who have never experienced it. That's why I believe the very best people to help addicts through their journeys are fellow travellers, those who have walked that same path and know all the potholes and wrong turns. Addicts will be able to walk that path with fellow travellers, they will respect them for the experience they have suffered, and they may be more willing to listen to advice from them that is not easy to hear. I believe it's harder for other counsellors to gain that respect, no matter how well-meaning or educated they are. There are some brilliant trained counsellors, but when I had counselling, I always knew my counsellor had never experienced the things I had. This is probably why so many recovered addicts make such brilliant professional counsellors, just as counsellors who have experienced bereavement or divorce are able to empathize with those they counsel, who are going through the same issues.

I accept that many recovering addicts may feel ashamed of their addiction and, once they have turned their back on their old life, they feel no calling to help others. That is fine. But for those of you who have travelled the path and want to reach out and help others, I would encourage you. You have a powerful testimony that will offer hope. You will also benefit personally in terms of your own recovery journey. Addicts need to know there is hope when they feel none exists. That's what makes the message of a recovering addict such a strong one to those still suffering.

There are several brilliant Christ-based recovery courses you can get involved in. Celebrate Recovery, the brilliant eight-week Release Course offered by Christians Against Poverty (CAP), and The Recovery Course are just three examples. There are more details at the back of this book. If there isn't a course near you, why not pray about starting one?

Every group leader on The Recovery Course I lead must have:

- a close relationship with God
- experienced an addiction
- found recovery through Christ
- a desire to help others.

Because the leaders have themselves experienced addiction, they have an instant rapport with those still struggling; a bond, an empathy that naturally engenders trust.

We are called to a life of action, and helping others is one way to express our faith and show our love. James, the half-brother of Jesus, writes, "What good is it, dear brothers and sisters, if you say you have faith but don't show it by your actions? Can that kind of faith save anyone?" (James 2:14). We need to show love for others by taking action, not just talking about it. I am also convinced we need to be out in the real world and not just surrounded by our holy huddle of Christian friends and only attending Christian events.

However, there is a danger that we, as recovering addicts, become so focused on helping others that we forget that our own recovery is a journey, and we can think we have arrived at our destination, often with disastrous effects. It then becomes very hard to put our hands up and admit we slipped up. We know it's a spiritual battle, and helping others puts us right on the front line. Standing up in our trench to help pull someone up means we are exposed to enemy fire. It's much safer and far more effective to stay on their level – to remember that we are addicts too – than to stand on a pedestal and try to pull them up.

Helping others is a wonderful privilege, but one that demands complete honesty. We need to accept that recovery is a gift; it's not earned. We also need to accept that, as recovered or recovering addicts, we are still addicts and we always will be.

Even as I write this book, I am reminded that my own recovery is a gift of grace, and I have to take each day at a time. We need to remain humble so the power of our Lord and his gift of grace can work through us to help others. It's not our knowledge, our willpower, the positive thinking we display through our cognitive behaviour patterns. It's the fact that we see that we are weak and accept the gift of recovery. As St Thomas Aquinas put it, "God is so powerful that he can direct any evil to a good end." The best example I can think of for how not to help others is the annoying way many ex-smokers look down on those who still smoke as though they are weaklings, forgetting the years of torment they went through before they eventually quit. If we don't get alongside those who are still struggling, if we look down on them, we won't be much help to them, and we put our own recovery at risk. If you have found recovery as you have read this book, please, please, keep taking it one day at a time, and keep looking up at the light.

In the next chapter we will look at the practical ways we can deal with the addiction voice.

Review
God uses all our experiences, good and bad. As recovering addicts we can be a great help to those still in active addiction. Not only that, but the act of helping others helps us too.

Exercise

- Pray about ways you could help those still in addiction, Christians and non-Christians.

- Write your testimony and be prepared to tell it.

- Research whether there is a Christ-based recovery course near you. Could you help? Could you attend? Could you start one up?

- Don't feel guilty if you are not ready to help others; just be open to a future calling.

CHAPTER 13

Dealing with the Addiction Voice

*So, dear brothers, you have no obligations whatever to your old sinful
nature to do what it begs you to do. For if you keep on following it you
are lost and will perish, but if through the power of the Holy Spirit
you crush its evil deeds, you shall live.*

Romans 8:12–13 (Living Bible)

For three horrible years, I woke with a sense of guilt followed by
shame for the money I had squandered and the time I had wasted
chasing my losses. I felt regret for all the lies and the deceit of
covering up my habit. On many occasions, in a moment of clarity,
I promised myself I wouldn't bet that day. I convinced myself that
this day would be the day I stopped; this day would be the first
day I started to get my old life back. And then I heard a voice.
It sounded so plausible. First it asked me how I was going to get
enough money to pay the bills that month. It asked me how I was
going to cover my tracks. That voice crushed what little hope I had
managed to muster. Throughout the morning the same small voice
incessantly pestered me until in the end it was a roaring shout telling
me to find the £50 I needed to back a team, a horse, or a tennis
player who was bound to win that afternoon. I let that voice in, I let
it speak, and I listened – because I had no defence. My own pride
meant I had pushed God away. I had no armour to protect me from
the barrage of persuasion.

But there is a defence. We don't have to listen to the lies of the
addiction voice. In this chapter we will look at some of the practical
things we can do to block it out and to feel the freedom to make
logical decisions rather than insane ones.

If we accept that our recovery journey is a spiritual battle, then our mind is the battlefield. It is the place where both sides meet and engage. In warfare, the front line is a messy place, but it is where decisive battles take place, where breakthroughs are made and the war is won.

I met Mike, a guy in his twenties. I had been invited to speak at a private function after dinner in a smart seafront hotel on the south coast. While all the guests were seated in the room enjoying a lovely buffet supper, I slipped outside to gather my thoughts. That's when I saw him. He was waiting outside the room, looking rather nervous. I struck up a conversation. He told me he had been invited by a friend and didn't want to go inside until the speaker started to talk. Mike had a gambling habit which was out of control, and he told me he had only come because a well-meaning friend had dragged him along, but he was certain that nothing any speaker was going to say would help him. He was lost and he felt no hope. He told me he hated gambling, but he knew that before the next day was over he would be back in the bookies playing roulette on the machines. He said he hated himself because when the day started, he'd make a promise not to bet. But then he would hear a voice that would persuade him that today would be different, today he would win big and be able to pay off all his debts. It would tell him his life was miserable and he had nothing more to lose. Debt was dragging him down. He had long since lost any self-respect, but he recognized that he still had too much pride to accept help. He wasn't sure he would even listen to the talk. He wanted to "stay on his toes", which was why he was outside, so he could make a dash if he wanted to.

The voice Mike heard each day is the same voice I listened to for three years. I call it the addiction voice. The things it says are lies, but they are also incredibly plausible, and often exactly what we want to hear at that moment in time. The real danger is that the addiction voice is so devious, it sounds like our own.

Mike stayed for the talk. Afterwards, I asked if there were any questions. Mike's hand shot up first. He wanted to know what it felt like to be free, free from debt and constant temptation. He wanted some hope so he could win the battle he has each day in his mind. I have no idea if the talk helped him, but we had a chance to pray together afterwards and he promised to stay in touch.

Mike, like me when I was in the depth of my own addiction, could see no light at the end of the tunnel. There is hope, there is freedom, there is an alternative to giving in, and an alternative to the bleak prospect of self-willed abstinence, to white-knuckle riding.

The sole aim of the devil is our destruction. In Revelation 12:9, the Bible describes him as "the one deceiving the whole world". He doesn't like it when we find joy and peace through a relationship with Christ, when we turn our backs on darkness and start to live in the light. It makes us a target. When we experience intimacy in our relationship with Christ, when we are spiritually healthy and have regular times when we listen to God through his word and talk to him through prayer, we are living in the light. But if we begin to have secret habits and tolerate sin, we allow darkness in and become vulnerable to attack.

This is nothing new. If we substitute the word "addiction" for "sin" and are prepared to be honest, we would all benefit from accepting the fact that we are all addicts; we are all addicted to sin. We just can't help it. Addiction is the same as everyday temptation; it's just that the outcome is more destructive, for us and for those around us. But we don't need to tolerate it or allow it to take over our lives. We have been forgiven once and for all. Christ's death gives us the victory; we just need to claim the freedom that victory gives us. It may take time, but the victory is ours nonetheless.

It is always a gentle slope. For me, the sin I tolerated was pride. I thought I had made it in life. I began to believe in my own talents and stopped leaning on God. As I have said, my morning Bible study and my prayer time dried up. I stopped going to church. I became vulnerable. We then have a choice. We can repent and turn back to God, at which point the devil flees. Or we can allow our sin to separate us from God, in which case the devil gets a foothold. Humility is what is required – the opposite of pride. When we realize it is our choice either to repent and turn back to the light or to allow our pride to tolerate sin, then we are empowered to claim victory through Christ by making the right decision. It's not the devil that defeats us. As children of God, we have the victory; it's our own openness to sin that defeats us. That means we have the key to victory. There is hope; there is a choice.

The devil knows this, so he uses the addiction voice to deceive us by saying, "You are worthless. God can't forgive you. You've screwed your life up already, so you have nothing to lose. Anyway, it will make you feel better."

First the voice pulls us down, sapping our strength, removing our hope, and leaving us open to depression. Then it reduces our self-respect. But somehow it manages to do this without taking away our pride. So although we condemn ourselves as idiots, we won't accept being told we are by anyone else, and we will try all we can to make it look as though we are holding it together. Then, when our defences are down, the voice tells us we will feel much better if we escape from the painful place by using, by medicating, by comfort eating, by shopping, or by placing a bet, or by any other substance or process that alters our mood and helps us temporarily forget about our misery. It's a quite ruthless and vicious tactic, and leads into a downward spiral towards depression and self-destruction.

So how can we defeat this voice in our head? How can we break the cycle? For me, the voice went very quiet when I made it captive to Christ and made the choice not to use. Our addictions may be deeply entrenched and we can give a whole list of reasons for using, such as resentment and hurt, the fear, the boredom, the way it helps us to cope with loneliness or stress, or just life in general. But we use because we enjoy it in some way, or so the deceiver tells us. Whatever our excuse, we still have a choice to use or abstain. That choice is given to us by our maker, and although I do believe he can and will heal us, we still have to make that choice.

I made that choice on a day when I had been completely humiliated. With five months' rent owing, I was told I was about to be evicted from a house which had once been a happy family home. While my mother, my wife, and my brother looked on, I collected up what possessions I hadn't sold to fund my habit into a black bin liner, and I left that house a broken man. It was just what I needed, because it broke my pride. Without pride I confessed my sin and asked God to mend me. I chose not to be an addict any more. Removed from the place where I indulged my habit, I was reminded of it less, I had fewer triggers (familiar images, places, behaviours, feelings that became linked to my habit and caused the voice to lie to me about using). Although it was painful, leaving that house had many practical benefits. Maybe you have friendships or routines that need to be changed.

When I did hear the voice, I took the advice of the apostle Paul when he urges us to "take captive every thought to make it obedient to Christ" (2 Corinthians 10:5, NIV UK). This is how we can deal with the voice – or if you prefer to call it temptation, that's fine:

- Recognize it and accept it is not our own voice, but that of the deceiver.
- Understand that the things it tells us are lies and that its advice is destructive and will have the opposite outcome to the appealing result it assures us of.
- Be firm with it and do not entertain it. Do not engage, reply, or even listen to it.

The deceiver is ruthless at using our thoughts and our senses (particularly our eyes) to generate strong feelings that persuade us that indulging our compulsive behaviour of choice would be a good thing. As I have said, the deceiver makes us think that the persuasive voice is our own. Don't listen to it; don't engage with it. It will always have the most persuasive reason, and if you listen to it you will start to get excited in anticipation. Just cut it off, the earlier the better. Recognize it for what it is, pray about it, give it to Christ, and do something else. Call someone, go for a walk, do some exercise, go to your favourite verse: develop a strategy to deal with it – any strategy – but never, never, never talk to it other than to tell it to go away. Don't allow it to talk to you.

The less we listen to the voice, the less often it will talk to us. "So humble yourselves before God. Resist the devil, and he will flee from you" (James 4:7). Look at the first part of that verse. It's that word "humble" again, the opposite of proud. First remove the pride, then the devil will flee. I really love the use of the word "flee" here. I have a vivid picture of someone sprinting away from me, not just grudgingly and reluctantly turning their back!

The next verse is also wonderful: "Come close to God, and God will come close to you." It doesn't matter how far we have strayed, God is right there if we seek him. One of the lies the voice will tell us is that God will be angry and won't be able to forgive us. But the truth is that he does love us, he will forgive us, and he longs for our company again. We just need to be humble and then make the choice to resist the devil and turn to God.

In 2 Timothy 2:22, we see how it works both ways. We can really put some space between us and the devil if he is fleeing from us and we are running as well, in the opposite direction. As Paul urges his younger prodigy, "Run from anything that stimulates youthful lusts. Instead, pursue righteous living, faithfulness, love, and peace." In the same verse, Paul advises Timothy to "Enjoy the companionship of those who call on the Lord with pure hearts." Do you spend enough time with your Christian friends, with someone you are accountable to and honest with? Or are you surrounded by people who might encourage you to keep pursuing your habit?

Just one last piece of advice: if you have become chemically dependent and you make the decision to abstain, it is wise to let someone know you are detoxing in case there are complications and you feel ill in the early stages. I believe in the power of Christ to set us free; I also believe that God works through sound medical advice!

On The Recovery Course we have a whole session on dealing with the addiction voice. It includes a workshop where we go through a series of questions that give us practical tools. It's all about learning to recognize the voice for what it really is, and learning techniques to address it and close it down. I would encourage you to seek treatment, find a Christ-based recovery course near you, an Anonymous fellowship, or some counselling. If you need support, it is available and there is a list at the end of this book. Addiction is a lonely place, but your recovery is best shared.

The next chapter is written for those who suffer because of our addictions.

Review
The addiction voice is like any temptation. It seeks to deceive you into thinking it would be good to use. Don't listen to it, make it captive to Christ by not listening, and turn back to God.

Exercise and coping strategies

- Begin to recognize the voice and to accept that it is not your voice at all, but that of the deceiver.

- Think about some of the lies the voice likes to tell you, some of the things it makes you feel. Write them down each time you hear them. For example, the devil might say you are condemned by God, broken-hearted, unfairly judged, without hope, angry, afraid, anxious, guilty, discouraged, lonely, powerless, or broken. For each of these feelings or lies, find a verse of God's truth from the Bible and be ready to quote it back. It may take time to find the most appropriate verse for you, but time looking through God's word at all his promises is never wasted and will leave you feeling uplifted. You will feel empowered. The lies will be exposed.

- Find a strategy to help you ignore the voice. Maybe you can call a friend, do an activity, go for a walk, or do some exercise. You could listen to your favourite song, or read something. Don't engage with the voice other than to quote back the truth.

- An exercise that helped me, and still does, is to recognize that when the addiction voice tells me "I" want something that I know deep down will be destructive or wrong, I remind that voice that in fact, " 'I' don't want to do it; 'you' do. Go away." Be firm with it and it will flee!

- Do you have any friendships or routines that are unhealthy and cause you to trip up? Be ruthless. Take drastic action.

CHAPTER 14

How Can I Help an Addict, and What About Me?

A recent study that suggests for every problem gambler, on average there are nine other people adversely affected by their addiction. These might include partners, parents, children, and work colleagues. They are very often forgotten. But their pain is not self-inflicted, and it must be so hard to watch as a loved one harms themselves, and to be dragged down by their whirlwind of self-destruction. I have come to see how much my mother went through as she watched me self-destruct. My wife did the right thing to take our children and leave me. In my selfishness, I thought it was all about me. I didn't stop to think about the effect it was having on my family in the short term, nor how it might affect them in the years to come. Addiction is highly selfish, and the tragedy is that the ones we love are the ones we hurt the most.

A few years ago I read shocking stories and watched the news as teenage binge drinking was rated as one of the biggest problems in our society. I wondered how it would be as a parent if my children were to get into trouble by drinking too much. Now, however, research suggests that it is not our young people who are most at risk from drinking too much. It is the older generation, for whom opening a bottle of wine and finishing it every night of the week is normal. Our young people seem to know how destructive and dangerous that kind of behaviour is. Many of them come back from the gym or an exercise class in the evening and secretly worry that their parents or grandparents are drinking much more than is good for them. Maybe it makes some children sad, scared, or worried.

In this chapter I share some practical advice for those who are not addicts but who live with addiction every day. It's for the grandparent whose grandchild has been sent to prison because of their addiction. It's for every husband or wife, parent, son, daughter, or best friend who watches every day as someone they love harms themselves through addiction. You have to pick up the pieces and deal with the fallout when no one else will.

I frequently see a certain type of person at recovery. They don't tend to stay long. They arrive a little late. If they share, they don't empathize. They don't see themselves as an addict; they don't see their habit as a problem. They still feel they can control it. They keep checking their watch, and I know they won't be back next week. They are only here because someone who loves them wanted them to come. Their habit is causing someone else a problem. But they don't think the problem is their own.

These are the people who are still in denial. They came to the meeting to make someone else feel better, or to put a stop to their nagging. Maybe their loved one has just found out about their habit and persuaded them to take action. Maybe their loved one is fed up with the destructive behaviour and gave the addict an ultimatum: "Get help or I will leave you." It's harder if the addict is your child, because you can't ever leave them. You carry the pain with every step they take.

The conversation, when the loved one gets back from a recovery class, probably goes something like this: "I gave it a go, but I'm not nearly as bad as them. Having listened to the others, there's no way I'm an addict. If you think I have a problem, phew, you should listen to some of them! I don't think it really helped me at all, but I'm glad I went. At least I know I'm OK."

You can't fix the addict unless they want to be fixed.

I received a text message from a lady whose friend is an alcoholic.

She was planning to take her friend to the next Recovery Course. The message explained how sad she was when her friend said she didn't want to come. "I'm gutted; I tried so hard, but I can't make her come on the course."

This advice will be so very hard, but sometimes the only thing to do is nothing. It may be really clear to you that your friend, husband, wife, son, or daughter has a problem and they need help. But until that person is ready to seek help, the best thing you can do for them is to show them love and to pray.

Addicts can be hugely creative and manipulative. They might make you feel like it's your fault. There will be a strong temptation to cover up for them or make excuses for them. These are reasonable coping mechanisms that allow you to avoid confrontation, arguments, and abuse, but they will also enable them to continue to indulge their habit. This is a complex area and the accommodating way you respond to your loved one's behaviour may be the only way to make life manageable. However, you may be creating an environment that allows the addict to indulge their habit, creating a dysfunctional codependency that is hugely destructive. If this is something you are experiencing, I would urge you to seek help outside the family unit.

I know I was the most stubborn of all. I pushed everyone away. But with my pride finally out of the way, I responded to the love my mother showed me. She didn't judge me, lecture me, or even micromanage my time. We just put some blocks in place, agreed a few rules, and she trusted me to find recovery.

The second most helpful thing I can think of is to keep talking. Not in a repetitive, nagging way, but do cultivate an open dialogue. If you are worried about someone you love, bring the conversation round to a habit you might suspect they have. If they talk about it openly, then things are probably fine. If they clam up, or you know they are lying to you, then there may be an issue. Don't push too hard at this stage. If someone in your family has a habit, it needs to be brought out into the light. If it remains a secret, it can get worse.

If it is openly talked about, what is acceptable and unacceptable can be naturally established. I believe Emma suspected I had a habit, but I avoided conversations. I turned things around on her and it led to confrontation. Emma and I both hate confrontation, so we let it become a secret. Sometimes you have to confront the issue, but expect the addict to appear to have all the answers. Addicts can be devious and highly convincing. You shouldn't feel guilty or to blame if they choose not to share, but likewise, don't pretend there is nothing wrong.

You may feel worried or upset by their habit but you don't want to know the truth. Maybe you are doing something wrong yourself and you don't want to point the finger for fear of a finger being pointed back at you. If that's the case, be careful: you are complicit and the issue is a codependency one – you just gave your husband or your wife permission to keep using, and they give you permission in return. It's all done on a subliminal level, but it is so destructive. Once again, you may need help; don't suffer alone.

I really don't want to make you paranoid, and often there is a really good reason for certain behaviour that doesn't mean your loved one is an addict, but I guess you are reading this chapter because you are already worried. It is so much better to recognize a behaviour pattern before it becomes an addiction. Once it is a full-blown compulsion, the extreme behaviour may be hidden from you and harder to break free from. Catch it early and agree what is acceptable and unacceptable. Prevention is so much better than cure. Here are some things to look out for. If you see any of these habits in someone in your family, talk to them about it. If they are:

- unusually withdrawn
- prone to mood swings: overly happy at times, depressed at others
- unusually secretive
- no longer open about internet use or finances
- no longer doing things they once loved to do
- giving you elaborate excuses about small things

- missing time from work or no longer socializing as much
- frequently late or unusually unreliable
- no longer exercising
- eating mints or chewing gum more often than usual, especially in the morning or early afternoon.

Chemical addictions are easier to spot in the long run because there are physical side effects, while process addictions may be harder to spot. If you know your loved one has particular character traits such as a full-on or addictive personality, if they are overly competitive, or faddy (they pick up hobbies and buy all the gear, only to lose interest after a few weeks), if they are optimistic, or unable to settle for one glass of wine, or one portion, then just be more alert. I am not saying people with these characteristics will form addictions, only that they may be more susceptible given the right circumstances, such as a painful situation, stress, worry, a redundancy, or a bereavement.

If there is a painful experience, such as when my eleven-month-old son almost died in my arms, make sure you both deal with the pain and try to stick together in the way it is dealt with. If you have a partner who doesn't like to talk, who bottles up worry, try to find a way to pop the cork with love and sensitivity. You may not be able to, and please don't feel guilty if you can't. Remember we can't change people unless they choose to change, but understanding that your partner is keeping stuff inside may help you both to deal with it. I know Emma tried, but I hid so much from her.

Love and sensitivity are the two key words in knowing how to deal with addiction in someone you care about. It's not easy because you will have your own anger, resentment, betrayal, hurt, fear, and anxiety to deal with, through no fault of your own. However, I do know that unless you can show some empathy, it will make matters worse. I guess what I am trying to say is, don't feel responsible, but don't heap on the guilt, and equally, don't give permission for the addictive behaviour to continue as an open "secret".

I have two more words of advice. The first is, please try to remember that while addiction is selfish, it doesn't mean the addict doesn't love you. Their actions will be illogical, maybe even insane at times. They will be hurtful, and you will rightly feel they don't care about you. The truth is that I did care and I never stopped loving my wife or children. As I began to hate myself because of my addiction, I found it harder to show love. Please don't even try to apply logic to an addict and their behaviour.

The last thing to say is that you also need love and support. The emphasis always seems to be on the recovery of the addict, their needs, and their support. What about yours? You will be much more of a help to your loved one if you are receiving the care you need. You may feel totally isolated and alone, not knowing where to turn, not wanting to reveal a terrible secret, but I want to encourage you to seek help for yourself. There are some great support groups around, and many of the Anonymous fellowships have "Anon" groups for those affected by the behaviour of addicts. Avoid the ones that provide a hate forum for the evil addict; find a place where you can openly express how you feel and where those listening will instinctively understand. Consider finding a counsellor, or at the very least a sympathetic friend.

Review
You can't fix an addict unless they are willing. Their actions may be hurtful and illogical, but they still love you. Try to encourage open discussion; don't condemn, but equally don't be complicit. You also need care and someone to talk to.

Exercise

- If you are worried or concerned, have that conversation with your loved one. Tell them how their habit makes you feel. Try to do it with sensitivity and love. Don't condemn, but be honest. Generate a healthy line of communication and don't give them permission to use by default.

- When you talk to them, let them know how their behaviour is affecting you. For example, say, "When you do this I feel…" rather than saying, "You do this all the time."

- If you believe there is a painful or stressful situation that your loved one is carrying – maybe you are too – then make sure it is dealt with. Don't ignore pain. Get some prayer, counselling, and support.

- Don't endure an addiction in a loved one on your own. You need somewhere and someone to share the pain and anger, the hurt and betrayal. Seek help and don't suffer alone.

CHAPTER 15

Alcohol

My child, listen and be wise:
Keep your heart on the right course.
Do not carouse with drunkards
or feast with gluttons,
for they are on their way to poverty.

Proverbs 23:19–21

According to the NHS, in the UK around 9 per cent of men and 4 per cent of UK women show signs of alcohol dependence, or alcoholism. That means for 8,333,000 people, drinking alcohol has become an important, or sometimes the most important, factor in their lives, and they feel unable to function without it. Society as a whole has accepted that drinking too much is normal, even though alcohol-related injuries clog our hospital A & E departments (there were 1,008,850 alcohol-related hospital admissions in 2014), and it costs us a huge amount in policing drink-related crime and causes misery on the roads. Alcohol is almost condoned as a stress reliever, and yet there is huge and overwhelming evidence of the damage alcohol dependence causes to our bodies and our minds, not to mention the negative effect of dependence on relationships and our wallets.

Here are the facts, according to Alcohol Concern:[8]

- More than 9 million people in England drink more than the recommended daily limits, and this figure will grow now the medical profession has lowered the safety limits.

8   www.alcoholconcern.org.uk (accessed 18 March 2016)

- In England, in 2012 there were 6,490 alcohol-related deaths, a 19 per cent increase compared to 2001.
- Alcohol accounts for 10 per cent of the UK burden of disease and death, making alcohol one of the three biggest lifestyle risk factors for disease and death in the UK, after smoking and obesity.
- An estimated 7.5 million people are unaware of the damage their drinking could be causing.
- Alcohol misuse costs England around £21 billion per year in healthcare, crime, and lost productivity The most effective strategies to reduce alcohol-related harm from a public health perspective include, in rank order, price increases, restrictions on the physical availability of alcohol, drink-driving countermeasures, brief interventions with at-risk drinkers, and treatment of drinkers with alcohol dependence.
- Alcohol is 61 per cent more affordable than it was in 1980.

Despite the evidence, alcoholism is a hugely misunderstood disease, with varying degrees of dependency that may not even involve excessive consumption. Being dependent doesn't mean you need a shot of vodka before you clean your teeth.

According to drinkaware:[9]

> *If you find that you "need" to share a bottle of wine with your partner most nights of the week, or always go for a few pints after work, just to unwind, you're likely to be drinking at a level that could affect your long-term health. You could also be becoming dependent on alcohol. If you find it very difficult to ... relax without having a drink, you could have become psychologically dependent on alcohol. Physical dependence can follow ... withdrawal symptoms, such as sweating, shaking and nausea, when your blood alcohol level falls.*

---

9   www.drinkaware.co.uk (accessed 18 March 2016)

Early in 2016, the Chief Medical Officer said that research shows that any alcohol consumption comes with a risk. There has long been a belief that there was a "safe" level of alcohol consumption, but that has turned out not to be the case.

There are many references to alcohol in the Bible, and I refuse to take any moral high ground on this issue except to say that I know I am an addict and I have to be careful with processes and substances that are highly addictive. I know I could so easily replace one addiction with another unless I let Christ deal with the issues inside me that make me want to use. Alcohol is incredibly addictive, both as a chemical in itself and also for the effect it has either to numb a painful situation or to celebrate a happy one. I also know how fresh I feel, how healthy and clear-headed, when I abstain.

Your relationship with alcohol is between you and God, unless your use of the drug – and that's what it is – affects others as well. Whatever your relationship with alcohol, it is worth remembering that alcohol is an "enabling" drug. It leads us to use other drugs or to take risks or to sin in ways we wouldn't have if we had been sober. I once used my company corporate card to place several bets, after I had stayed up all night with a couple of bottles of wine. Those bets caused more destruction to my life than any other. I am not sure I would have placed them if I had not been drinking.

Maybe alcohol lowers your defences against temptation and causes you to visit unhealthy websites which can lead to further sin. It's not the alcohol that is sinful, but giving in to the temptation it can lead to is. Jesus tells us to take a ruthless approach to anything that causes us to sin in Matthew 5:30 when he says, "And if your hand – even your stronger hand – causes you to sin, cut it off and throw it away." Better, I think, to avoid too much alcohol than to cut off our hands.

I could fill the pages of this book with a discussion on alcohol dependency. But here are some of the things I feel are important. There are no right or wrong answers to the questions below, only your own truthful ones:

- Don't be condemned. Drinking alcohol is not sinful in itself. Just be aware of the issues around it.
- It's not just about your consumption. Your example is also important, particularly if you have children.
- Could you use the money you spend on alcohol more effectively?
- Is your use affecting your physical health or your mental well-being? Is the high it might give you always followed by a low? Perhaps you don't feel like going to the gym the next day.
- Does alcohol improve your social life and relationships, or damage them?
- Is there a history of dependency on alcohol in your family? If so, be careful.
- Do you reach for a glass if you feel stressed, hungry, happy, angry, lonely, or tired?
- Do you drink every day or have periods when you stop?
- Have you ever set yourself a target of stopping or cutting back and failed to stick to it?
- Has your consumption of alcohol led to or caused you to use other drugs or sin?

Read through the following two stories with an open mind and see how they make you feel.

A bad day

It's been a long day. London is uncomfortably hot and my mind has been focused all day on the development of a new set of questions for a financial exam. Now my mind is numb. I've been paid well for my time, but I'm tired, hungry, and thirsty. I'm also a bit angry because my train is late, and for every minute it's delayed, more commuters crowd the platform, making it less likely that I will get a seat. I'm not much looking forward to arriving home to an empty house either: it's half term and Emma has taken the boys to see her parents. I'll be alone all week.

There is a bar at one end of the platform. Young, well-dressed executives are drinking cold beers and chatting excitedly. That's when

I first realize a voice has been nagging at me since I walked out of the office. It's my addiction voice. It's so easy to listen to and makes so much sense. I can hear it now; it's saying, "Go on, you've had a tough day. You deserve a beer. It'll help you relax, take away that cross edge you're feeling. Satisfy that thirst. One beer never hurt anyone. If you catch the train after the next one you might get a seat. There's no one at home to smell the alcohol on your breath, so there won't be any argument."

The addiction voice sounds so plausible, so right. But I have a bit of reasoning to do first. "What about the swim I was going to have on the way home? What about the small group meeting at church? I can't turn up smelling of alcohol," I reply.

"Aw, you can swim in the morning; you've been every day this week. The rest will do you good. And it won't hurt to miss the group tonight. They know how hard you work... Besides, with Emma away you can pick up a takeaway and watch your favourite TV show. No interruptions, maybe a glass of wine. You've worked hard; you deserve it."

The first beer goes down so fast I need another. Before I know it, I've missed the train. By the time I get home, I'm not at all sure it is legal for me to drive. I curse myself for taking such a stupid risk, but swing by the Chinese takeaway anyhow. It's right next to the off-licence. They always are.

The next morning I wake up late. I don't have time for the swim I promised myself. Besides, I have a headache. I don't even have time to read my Bible notes. Having missed my quiet time, I feel too guilty to pray on the train to work. I was meant to prepare for my first meeting, but I know I haven't and it goes badly wrong. In fact, the whole day goes badly and I find myself thinking it would be a good idea to escape the stress I feel. With my defences down and feeling short on self-esteem, I don't even bother arguing with my addiction voice. It's so hot and the train is late again. What shall I do?

A good day

It's been a long day. London is uncomfortably hot and my mind has been focused all day on the development of a new set of questions for a financial exam. Now my mind is numb. I've been paid well for my time, but I'm tired, hungry, and thirsty. The train is late, but I have come prepared. I put my headphones on and find a song I like. I don't feel so angry now. Instead of seeing the bar at the end of the platform, I walk to the other end of the station where the sun is shining and catch a few rays on my face. I've been inside an office all day, so I enjoy the warmth and let the music wash over me. Few people have ventured this far down the platform, so when the train arrives, I'll get a seat.

The train was a bit late, but I still have time to swim before my small group meeting. I was feeling a bit tired and not really looking forward to the small group, but after the swim I feel refreshed and make myself a healthy sandwich before I go out.

I'm so glad I made it to the group because someone there needed to talk to me about something that's been on their mind for a while. I drive home with a smile on my face and enjoy a couple of rather sleepy minutes of prayer over a hot chocolate in bed, and even a couple of pages of a novel. The sheets feel clean and soft, and before I know it I'm asleep.

After a refreshing night, I wake early and enjoy my quiet time. I pray about the day and take time to prepare for my business meeting. Today will be even better than yesterday.

We need to change our perspective if want to avoid being a slave to every craving or compulsive desire we feel, and to silence the addiction voice. Yes, we can manage it temporarily by understanding our triggers, by recognizing situations when we are most vulnerable (for me it's generally when I am hungry, happy, angry, lonely, or tired – HHALT). But we can't do it on our own or for the rest of our lives, because that's the way we have been programmed. We will be slaves to ourselves and our desires, to our appetites, unless we allow the love of God to change our perspective from within.

Paul sums it up to perfection in Romans 12:2: "Don't copy the behavior and customs of this world, but let God transform you into a new person by changing the way you think. Then you will learn to know God's will for you, which is good and pleasing and perfect." The battleground is the mind.

Paul wrote this version of "psychotherapy" 2,000 years before a very clever psychologist came up with cognitive behavioural therapy. We need to allow Christ to transform us from within and to give us a different perspective from that of the world around us. I know I will never "need a drink", despite what my addiction voice tells me!

In the next chapter we will look at some of the issues related to eating disorders.

Review

Alcoholism is widespread and its negative effects on our health are well known. And yet, as a society, we take a tolerant view on the use of alcohol. When abused, alcohol is an enabler and a gateway to other habits. It is also highly addictive. When did you last have an honest conversation about your relationship to alcohol with God and/or a friend?

Exercise

- Buy a notebook and keep account of your alcohol consumption at home over two weeks. Alternatively, place your empties in a box and keep them.

- At the end of two weeks, calculate the cost of your alcohol and work out the number of units you have consumed. Take a trip to one of the alcohol advice pages (such as www.drinkaware.co.uk) and compare your consumption to the safe guidelines.

- Did you notice any patterns in your use? For example, do you have a drink when you are stressed, or when you cook, or when you are with certain friends? Think about your patterns.

- Have an honest talk with God. What would he say to you about your consumption?

- Take a break. Even if you drink a little each day, have a day or two regularly when you drink nothing. Try to do it for a month and see how you feel. Give alcohol to God as a gift.

- If you can't keep to self-imposed limits, you may need to treat your use of alcohol as an addiction and seek some help or advice. There is plenty available through your GP.

  Warning: If you decide to abstain and you know you are a heavy user, tell someone you are detoxing. You may experience the shakes, nausea, or sweating. If this is the case, you have probably formed a physical/chemical addiction to alcohol and you do need to seek help.

CHAPTER 16

Eating Disorders

So whether you eat or drink, or whatever you do, do it all for the glory of God.

1 Corinthians 10:31

Sophie was only thirteen when a girl said something to her that she would carry with her for the rest of her life. It was just a throwaway comment, but it had a huge impact. Her parents sent Sophie to one of the top private boarding schools in the country, but she was missing home and finding it hard to fit in. She already had a feeling that she just wasn't as good at anything as the other girls.

They were changing for a gym lesson when one of the popular girls looked over at Sophie. Almost as an accusation, she said, "You couldn't even be anorexic."

It was just a few words, but something snapped inside Sophie's head. From that moment on, she became determined that she *would* be anorexic; she would show the other girls that she could do something well. She began to eat less, and when she did eat, she would frequently sneak off and make herself sick. She began to exercise compulsively, until her weight dropped to dangerous levels. At first she was trying to make herself thin, but after a while it became a habit. It gave her comfort from the reality of the world. She stopped communicating, and she had no self-esteem.

Then one day, in her twenties, she just woke up, looked back, and wondered where the last twelve years had gone. Sophie became a Christian, and for the first time she felt she was loved. It gave her the power to make the decision to shed her comfort blanket and face up to the real world. It was hard at first, because she had to deal with life for the first time instead of hiding from it.

I spoke to Sophie recently. She told me she has turned her back on her eating disorder, but she still feels the pain of that incident in the changing room. Even now, when anyone says something unkind, or even just thoughtless, she is instantly taken back to that life-changing moment.

If we can abstain from our habits, after a time our body begins to forget the pathways and triggers that once wired us. We can move on and it becomes easier to abstain. But there is one habit we will never be able to abstain from and, for those who struggle with it, one habit we will always face: eating. In the UK, it is estimated that more than 1.6 million people struggle with anorexia or bulimia. However, the Department of Health believes that the true figure could be as high as 4 million people because many never seek help or even admit they have a problem. A further 15 million people are obese, often as a result of compulsive eating through stress or anxiety. Binge eating disorders and emotional overeating are common, where the "drug" is food and the pain we escape from is emotional.

Overeating, often in search of comfort and escape, is the second most serious lifestyle risk factor leading to death and disease. Obesity is a greater threat than alcoholism, and second only to smoking as the most lethal.

According to the NHS, anorexia nervosa is a serious mental health condition. It is an eating disorder where those who suffer have a strong desire to lose weight. They usually do this by compulsively restricting the amount of food they eat, making themselves vomit, and exercising excessively. The condition often develops out of anxiety about body shape and weight that originates from a fear of being fat or a desire to be thin. Many people with anorexia have a distorted image of themselves, thinking that they're fat when they're not. Or it can be about wanting to have some control, particularly for teenagers who feel they have no control in any other area of their lives.

Anorexia most commonly affects girls and women, although it has become more common in boys and men in recent years. Reports suggest as many as 25 per cent of those suffering from eating disorders are male, and this figure is growing. On average, the condition first develops at around the age of 16 to 17. Those suffering often feel ashamed and go to great lengths to hide their habit. They lie about what they have eaten, or pretend they have already eaten in order to avoid meals. Those I have spoken to say they feel trapped.

Help is available, but the key, as with all these issues, is to realize you have a problem. It may have been a habit you have lived with and hidden for many years and so it may seem quite normal for you.

If you suspect someone has an eating disorder, just like any other addiction, talk to them and try to encourage them to open up. And like any other addiction, until they realize they have a problem and want to get better, recovery won't start. The conversation may be difficult. They may become defensive or deny there is any problem. If you suspect someone you know has a problem with anorexia or any other eating disorder, the NHS has identified some signs to look out for:

- missing meals, eating very little, or avoiding any fatty foods
- obsessively counting calories in food
- leaving the table immediately after eating so they can vomit
- taking appetite suppressants, laxatives or diuretics (medication that helps remove fluid from the body)
- repeatedly weighing themselves or checking their body in the mirror
- physical problems, such as feeling lightheaded or dizzy, hair loss, or dry skin.

Many of us obsess about our weight. You can see that every January when the gym is packed out. There are thousands of apps for our phones and computers that allow us to record every calorie, and it is easy to become obsessive. Just because you go on a diet or enjoy takeaway food doesn't mean you have an eating disorder, so please don't read this and feel condemned. But if you genuinely have an issue, please seek help. There is a short self-diagnosis exercise at the end of this chapter. If you are worried, take time to prayerfully answer the questions.

Anorexia can also be associated with other psychological problems such as depression, anxiety, low self-esteem, alcohol misuse, and self-harm. If you recognize these issues, I would encourage you to visit one of the eating disorder support groups such as Beat.

Dealing with an eating disorder is the same as for any other habit. The important thing is to recognize you have an issue, talk about it, and seek help. I love food and I know I have to find balance in my life, both in terms of my diet and also the exercise I take. Like any other habit that damages our health, it may help to remember that our bodies are the temple of Christ, the dwelling place of the Holy Spirit. He doesn't want us to be compulsive about food; neither does he want us to develop a crippling disorder. A healthy respect for our health is required and is what Christ wants for us, because he wants us to be free and to enjoy life to the full.

Review

Nineteen million of us suffer from some form of eating disorder. That's almost one in three. Undereating or overeating are often ways to escape pain and can be used to protect ourselves from the emotional trials of life. But, at best, they drag us down, lower our self-esteem, and damage relationships. At their worst they are lethal for our health. The important thing is to recognize if there is an issue, talk about it, and seek help.

Exercise

Remember that most of us have issues with food from time to time. Don't feel guilty, but do answer these questions truthfully:

- Have you ever lied about your eating?

- Do you regularly experience guilt about what you eat, and do you feel disgusted or depressed afterwards?

- Have you ever experienced a feeling that you lacked control over your eating, particularly while you were eating?

- Have you eaten alone because you are embarrassed?

- Have you binged on more than one occasion?

- Do you ever eat to alter your mood, even when you don't feel physically hungry?

- Have you ever made yourself sick after eating?

- Does it surprise you when other people comment on your weight loss?

- Are you obsessive about everything you eat, recording every calorie?

- Do you exercise for health reasons or are you trying to lose weight, even though you know your weight is healthy?

- Some questions are general, some relate to binge eating, and some to anorexia.

- If answering these questions makes you feel uneasy, talk to someone about it. Today.

CHAPTER 17

Pornography

"Your eye is like a lamp that provides light for your body. When your eye is healthy, your whole body is filled with light."

Matthew 6:22

"Hi Justyn, are you free for coffee this afternoon?" The call was from one of the young guys in our church. The church I am a member of has a really good mentoring programme. I have a mentor, a very wise man called Chris, but I guess someone thought that, as I had a bit of worldly experience, I might be able to help a younger Christian making his way in life too. My speciality is "How not to do it!"

"Yep, OK. Usual place? Did you want to discuss something specific?" I asked.

"Umm, no, not really, just a bit of a catch-up."

As I waited for him to arrive at the high street coffee shop, I wondered what Mark wanted to talk about. I was pretty sure there would be something in particular. I had a feeling I knew what that something was. But after twenty minutes of general catching up, I began to wonder. I looked at my watch and made an excuse about having to get back. As I stood up, I could see Mark still had something he wanted to ask, and the lack of eye contact convinced me that my first instinct was right.

"Well there is one other thing. I don't really know how to ask you. It's probably not important, but…"

"You want to know if I've ever had a problem with pornography?"

The relieved look on his face told me all I needed to know.

Mark is a student and brilliant with technology. He spends a lot of time on his laptop; he has a smart phone and a tablet. He also has a lot of spare time. He told me he found the website by accident. At first it was just an occasional look. But the first website led him to another, and another, and each one became more extreme, until he just didn't know what was normal any more. It was affecting his relationship with God and his relationship with his girlfriend; he was becoming more reclusive, and his studies were suffering.

The reality is that Mark's situation is not unusual. The facts show that 86 per cent of all males regularly access pornography on the internet, as do 36 per cent of women. A recent study of 2,000 Christians in church congregations in the UK and the US found that 73 per cent of men and 30 per cent of women had accessed pornography at least once in the previous month.

Accessing porn is a habit that becomes more extreme the more it is hidden. It is a habit that has tripped up many a church leader. They have the same urges as anyone else, but often spend prolonged time alone at their desks. Time and access are two dangerous commodities when it comes to temptation. A church pastor told me it was the most common reason for members of the congregation to make an appointment to see him. They are just the honest ones!

I sat down again and felt very sorry for Mark. When I was a student, the embarrassment of walking into a newsagent, reaching up to the top shelf, and taking an adult magazine to the till would have been enough to stop me from viewing explicit images. But now, according to Google, the most searched for word is "sex". I believe it can actually be harder to avoid internet pornography that to find it. Pop-ups, advertising, social media links, and hacked legitimate sites make steering clear more and more difficult.

The free and simple availability of pornography on the internet has generated a whole new industry worth billions. But at what price? Some say it is harmless, even good for you. But the reality is that it can damage relationships between men and women. Studies suggest that an increase in sexual assaults in schools is directly attributable to pornography. The revenues generated have led to an increase in modern-day slavery and sex trafficking, as many involved in slavery end up involved in this industry.

The long-term effects of internet pornography are yet to be fully established and are difficult to quantify, but one thing is for certain: like any sin, it damages our relationship with God. There is a whole range of addictions relating to sex. Any of you reading this who don't believe that the use of pornography really is an addiction should ask those who spend six hours at a time on the internet searching for more and more extreme images. Ask them how it affects their self-esteem.

One horrible feature of addiction is the way our appetites seem to grow. We have to drink more to get the same effect, bet bigger stakes, or use harder drugs. Pornography is the same, and eventually, if left unchecked, the appetite for it grows too, and leads to a place where children are abused and crimes are committed. I'm not saying that everyone who uses pornography is a paedophile; simply that something that is often seen as harmless fun does, at its most extreme, have an evil side to it.

Addictions to pornography develop over time. This is one of the process addictions rather than chemical, but when it comes to secret habits, especially among men, this is the big one. If dealt with early enough, though, it's not difficult to manage. If you leave it until it becomes a problem, you need to deal with it in the same way as any other addiction.

"What about your blocks, Mark?" I asked.

He looked at me as though I was talking about bits of wood.

"Your browser content filter managers."

Now I was speaking his language, but he looked surprised! "Can you do that?" he asked me.

Now I was surprised. Mark is a techno geek, and I am a caveman in comparison. I explained how he can block all adult content from his devices by the use of free browser filter software.

Covenant Eyes and K9 are really good. They are free and simple to install. I told Mark we could do it together and he should let me have the password, so he wouldn't be tempted to turn it off. We installed it on his laptop there and then, and arranged it so an email would be sent to me, the "administrator", if he tried to access anything he shouldn't have access to. It took us three minutes. By doing this, he agreed to be accountable to a fellow Christian, and I told him I had someone I was accountable to as well. He agreed to do the same for his tablet and his smartphone. Outside, we prayed together briefly, committing it to God. He seemed much happier when we parted.

When I talk to Christians who want to stop viewing internet pornography, male and female, they often tell me it's not difficult to get round browser blockers. But they do say that having someone they are accountable to, someone they meet every other week who will ask them if they have looked at anything they shouldn't, really helps them. They know they will either have to lie or admit their weakness again. It is a very powerful way of making something that can be so easy a lot more difficult to do. Mark did the right thing. He didn't want to keep sinning and he knew he had to bring his habit out into the light, to a place where God could deal with it and where Mark could take positive action.

The Lord knows we will sin, slip up, and do things we regret. He knew before we were born. We might see pornography as unimportant. To God, it is unacceptable and is something we need to take a firm stance against, the earlier the better. Block it out before it becomes a secret, stinking habit.

In the next chapter we will look at the issue of problem gambling. I am not proud to say that I know quite a lot about it.

Review
Pornography use is widespread, even in our church congregations, and it is harmful to us and to our relationship with God. Easy access to pornography can be controlled through browser filters.

All Christians should have a browser filter on their computers and adult content controls on their TVs.

Exercise

- Download Covenant Eyes or K9 and give the password to someone you trust.

- Set up your TV system and broadband with adult controls and filters.

- Find an accountability partner or buddy up with someone who will regularly ask about what you have been viewing and pray with you, and to whom you can give access as a browser blocker administrator.

CHAPTER 18

Compulsive Gambling

A hard worker has plenty of food,
but a person who chases fantasies ends up in poverty.
The trustworthy person will get a rich reward,
but a person who wants quick riches will get into trouble.

Proverbs 28:19–20

I didn't see it coming. I didn't know it would destroy my life. It looked harmless, a bit of fun. But for me and 560,000 other people in the UK, not to mention our families, it is misery.

Harmful gambling was medically recognized as a pathological compulsive addiction only in 2013. It remains one of the least understood addictions. Very little treatment is available, and hardly any preventative education. In fact, the positive aspects of gambling are heavily advertised. The negative aspects are rarely discussed, as recovering gamblers are reluctant to share their stories for fear of being misunderstood, judged, and stigmatized. It's almost acceptable to be an alcoholic, or a drug addict, but if you are a compulsive gambler you're just an idiot. Yes, there is only so much alcohol you can consume in one day, only so many times you can shoot up. For a gambler, the size of their habit is restricted only by the size of their bank account. Gambling addiction is no respecter of gender, age, or status. At its worst it is a killer, and it will frequently lead to a prison sentence if left unchecked.

Compulsive gamblers, however, are not stupid. Devious, calculating, resourceful, and selfish maybe; like other addicts, we are driven by an instinct that overrides all reason. It may look stupid from the outside, but it makes perfect sense to a gambler.

If you know someone who gambles compulsively, and the statistics suggest that you probably do, let me take you on a journey into their minds, just for a second or two. Firstly, a compulsive gambler is an optimist. He or she expects to win. If you are one of those people who buy a lottery ticket and lose it or forget to check your numbers, you probably don't have a problem. Even though the odds of winning are 45 million to one, a compulsive gambler expects to win the lottery and will have spent the days leading up to the draw planning how they will spend their money. They will be very generous to all their friends, of course, but in there will also be the new house, the flash car, the holiday. In my first book, *Tails I Lose*, I tell the story of a lady in the post office who takes her benefit cheque and buys twenty Benson and Hedges and 200 scratch cards. She would have been fantasizing about how to spend all her winnings. I hope she and her little daughter didn't go hungry that week. But they probably did.

Gambling is about adrenaline. It's about escapism. It is not about the money. It's a complex addiction because, although it is a process-based addiction, there is a chemical element as the risks get higher. At the height of my addiction I could easily place a thousand bets a day, mostly on the roulette table, and the adrenaline could keep me awake all night.

An American study recently linked gambling to mental illness. Some say gambling is an illness; others say that's just a way of deflecting responsibility. What I do know is that seeing it as an illness has helped many compulsive gamblers who are trying to come to terms with a horrible affliction. I am yet to meet a compulsive gambler who blames anyone other than themselves – if they genuinely want recovery.

A compulsive gambler will keep gambling when they lose because they are expecting to win. The problem is, it's a statistical probability that the more you gamble, the more you will lose. If they do win, they will keep playing because they convince themselves that they are on a winning run and "this time" they can win everything back. The override button is out of control and delusion has set in.

My greatest concern is for young people. They are the ones who are the most adept at smartphone technology; they are the ones who respond to the barrage of advertising surrounding televised sport. The 16- to 24-year-old age group represents the largest group calling the gambling helplines. Incidentally, these helplines are funded by the gambling industry, not the government, who takes hundreds of millions in revenue from the gambling industry each year. Research is also predominantly funded by the gambling industry. My concern is that there is no desire to publish the true figures.

A few months ago I came downstairs to find my 7-year-old son playing a fruit machine on his tablet. I was so shocked I grabbed it and found that he was just playing his favourite game, one where you build a fun park from scratch to attract visitors who "pay". The more credits you earn, the more exciting rides you can build. You can build fast-food outlets that also generate "income". I discovered that one of the things you can build is a casino. You can go inside and play slot machines where you can "win" more credits.

I did some research. The owner of the funfair game is a gambling company based in Las Vegas.

I believe that we are normalizing behaviour patterns that reward risk in our young people. Everything is made so easy. I am convinced we are storing up serious problems for future generations. I also worry about the advertising (which has no watershed control limitations), which specifically targets women, with fun-looking bingo and colourful jingles, "free" spins and excitement. Women often hold and manage the finances in the family, and those who are homemakers may have more spare time. The gambling industry marketing experts know this.

But what can a gambler who suspects they have a problem do about it? What if you suspect someone is gambling too much? It is hard to hide a drink or drug addiction, but gambling is easier to conceal. And if you are losing, you are probably spending more recklessly and will try to cover it up. Don't. Open up and talk about it. I left it until it was too late and it cost me my marriage. It's the lies and the deceit, the damage to trust, that are the problem.

Seek help. There may well be a Gamblers Anonymous group that meets regularly near you. Join one if you can. The same blocks that work for pornography work for gambling. Put them on all your devices. Be open about your finances, and ask someone you trust to review them regularly. This accountability with a friend works across the addiction range. In the fellowships, it is formalized in the Sponsor/Addict relationship. But you don't have to find someone who has themselves recovered from the same addiction; just someone who will offer you understanding and support. You can add their names to your account as a third-party mandate, or even ask your husband or wife to take over the finances and just give you what you need from day to day. Understand your triggers. If you regularly stop off at the same bookmakers on your journey home from work, take a different route and don't carry cash. If your habit is online, self-exclude. The betting companies have been forced to join a scheme where a gambler who recognizes they have a problem can self-exclude themselves from all the 2,500 online betting sites in one go. The scheme goes live in 2017. It's important to realize these blocks will not prevent anyone from placing a bet if they want to, but they may just provide a moment of clarity, giving the addict some time when they can choose to call someone or tell their addiction voice to go away. A huge problem is that it is so easy to place a bet, especially electronically when paying by credit card, and it just doesn't feel like money. Blocks make it harder. If you have hurdles to jump to place a bet, there is more chance you will come to your senses. It's about making it harder to do what the addiction voice is telling you to.

As a debt and addiction advisor, I see the damage a secret gambling habit can cause if left unchecked. Every day, I live with the consequences of my own habit. I visit people in prison and try to give hope where there is none. Gambling is a horribly destructive addiction, and the industry is honest enough to admit there are probably three and a half million people whose current gambling habits put them at risk in the UK.

As with any habit, the earlier it is brought out into the light, the less likely it is to become a full-blown destructive addiction. If you think you have a problem, talk to someone. If you suspect a problem in someone else, gently and sensitively talk to them. Tact is required, and the absence of a judgmental attitude, because the last thing anyone wants is for a habit to be driven underground.

Review
Compulsive gambling is poorly understood and intervention provision is scarce. There are steps that can be taken to block the habit, but the best way to manage a gambling habit is honesty and openness.

Exercise
If you are worried about your gambling, if you take time off work, spend more than you can afford or longer betting than you want to, if you gamble to escape worry or bet more to win back your losses, or if you can't keep to self-imposed limits, you may have a problem. If so:

- Call one of the gambling helplines. The number is in every betting shop and on every betting webpage.
- Talk about your concerns with a friend, partner, or someone you trust.
- Self-exclude, online or in the betting shop.
- Use browser protection software.
- Understand your triggers and change your routines.
- Give someone control or oversight of your finances.
- Look up the nearest Gamblers Anonymous group and give it a try.

CHAPTER 19

Financial Addictions and Buying Disorders

Don't store up treasures here on earth, where moths eat them and rust destroys them, and where thieves break in and steal. Store your treasures in heaven, where moths and rust cannot destroy, and thieves do not break in and steal. Wherever your treasure is, there the desires of your heart will also be.

Matthew 6:19–21

Kelly loved her daughter. She knew her daughter had been born with a disability, but that just made her love her even more. One morning, just after her daughter's twelfth birthday, she dropped her off at the special school, as she had done so many times before, just another ordinary day.

That lunchtime Kelly's daughter wasn't able to swallow a piece of meat and it became lodged. Although her helper was there with her and the school did all it could, she choked to death.

I can't even imagine the grief Kelly must have felt. Or what it must have been like to clear her daughter's room. But Kelly found a way to cope, to deal with her pain. She had an eBay account and had bought a few things online before. Now she found herself spending hours online looking for bargains, bidding for things she didn't need. Her husband became more and more concerned as their house began to fill up with bags of clothes that Kelly never even tried on. When the credit card bills became unmanageable, he sought help for her. Kelly was shopping compulsively and had lost control of her habit.

Kelly's addiction may sound extreme, but I don't think there are many of us who haven't, at one time or another, been tempted into a little retail therapy. This doesn't mean we have a buying disorder or a shopping addiction. But it does help us to understand the issue. Studies suggest that between 10 and 15 per cent of us are predisposed to compulsive buying in some way.

According to Shopaholics Anonymous, there are several different types of shopaholics:

- compulsive shopaholics who shop when they are feeling emotional distress
- trophy shopaholics who are always shopping for the perfect item
- shopaholics who want the image of being a big spender and love flashy items
- bargain seekers who purchase items they don't need because they are on sale
- bulimic shoppers who get caught in a vicious cycle of buying and returning
- collectors who don't feel complete unless they have one item in each colour or every piece of a set.

If we are dealing with an emotional issue, if we are depressed, or if we're just feeling bored or a little down, we can use shopping to lift our mood. This is because, in some of us, as we spend money or buy something we think we need or want, the brain releases endorphins and dopamine. These chemicals can be extremely addictive and, like gambling, if our behaviours become repetitive, our bodies will tell us we need the drug.

Any habit that involves spending money can and will lead to problems, either financial or relational. It can be hard to recognize if there is a genuine problem, as we all spend a little too much sometimes. Just because you go on a shopping spree doesn't make you a shopaholic. Most of us enjoy shopping and we have all made the occasional impulse buy, but if you have lost control of your shopping, you respond to adverts on TV and the internet even when you don't need the items, then you may have a problem. The resulting debt can cause relationship breakdown. Those who know they have a problem may well try to conceal it by hiding items, being secretive about finances, and lying about what they have spent.

There are some signs to look for, either in yourself or a loved one:

- spending more than they can afford
- shopping as a reaction to feeling angry or depressed
- shopping as a way to feel less guilty about a previous shopping spree
- harming relationships owing to spending or shopping too much
- losing control of the shopping behaviour.

This addiction is similar to gambling in that it leads to debt. It has become much easier to buy things from the comfort of our homes. The internet has made it easier to spend our money, and that means more of us are exposed to the danger of forming spending habits that are destructive. An addiction in this area, or any addiction or compulsive habit that involves spending money, can cause misery, both for the addict and their loved ones because of the financial harm of the resulting debt.

We are called to be good stewards of our money, and it is important that we make a budget and record what we spend. As a family, it is important that we are open and honest with our finances, and we should give from the very first part of our income. If this is an area where God is challenging you, there are some very good Christian stewardship courses available, and some great books have been written on the subject. The Bible refers to money and possessions 2,350 times, and many of Jesus' parables were about money. He knew we would have problems with money and the love of money. Like our health, our finances should be respected. What we do with our money is important to God. We need to get our relationship with money right and not use it to medicate our pain, or protect us from reality.

If you are in trouble financially, seek advice from a debt charity. Avoid debt management companies which charge for their service and could encourage you to pay back more than you can afford (as they can take a percentage from your creditors in return for repayments you make). Christians Against Poverty (CAP) offers a brilliant service and doesn't charge a penny. You can also find help at Step Change or the Citizens Advice Bureau. When it comes to debt, don't bury your head in the sand. The issue always gets worse if you don't act. It's never as bad as you think when you do.

Review
Repeatedly shopping and buying things in order to alter our mood can be addictive because of the chemical our brain secretes in some of us when we spend money. Buying disorder is poorly understood and is seen by many as the fault of the individual. But it can and does cause misery for those suffering. Talking about the issues with someone and admitting there is a problem are the first steps to recovery. Don't ignore debt.

Exercise

Remember that we all spend a little too much from time to time. But answer these questions truthfully:

- Do you shop when you feel angry or disappointed?
- Has overspending created problems in your life?
- Do you have conflicts with loved ones about your need to shop?
- While shopping, do you feel euphoric rushes or anxiety?
- After shopping, do you feel like you have just finished doing something wild or dangerous?
- After shopping, do you ever feel guilty or embarrassed about what you have done?
- Do you frequently buy things that you never end up using or wearing?
- Do you think about money almost all the time?

If you answered yes to many of these questions, you may have an issue with spending. If answering these questions makes you feel uneasy, talk to someone about it. Today.

CHAPTER 20

Social Media

Next the devil took him to the peak of a very high mountain and showed him all the kingdoms of the world and their glory. "I will give it all to you," he said, "if you will kneel down and worship me." "Get out of here, Satan," Jesus told him. "For the Scriptures say, 'You must worship the Lord your God and serve only him.'"

Matthew 4:8–10

"I'm really worried about Claire. She seems to be on her phone all the time. She doesn't communicate with us, even at mealtimes. When we try and talk about it, she just snaps at us. I can't take her phone away; she says it's how all her friends communicate. Her light was on till late last night. She had to go to school today so I went into her room and she tried to hide her phone from me. I have no idea what she is looking at or who she is talking to. I don't understand technology like she does. I don't do Facebook. I think it's causing her mood swings, and the lack of sleep is affecting her at school. I have no idea what to do."

I have had similar conversations with other concerned parents. I am one myself. I do know that social media, Facebook, Twitter, Instagram, and other social networking sites, have transformed the way we communicate and opened up opportunities for global forums. It has given many a worthy cause a new platform and led to some wonderful social reform. But can it cause harm; is it a problem for some?

Most people I talk to would never associate their use of social media with a discussion about addiction. And yet, Facebook Addiction Disorder (FAD) has become a recognized compulsive condition with an estimated 350 million people worldwide suffering because they have lost control. When our online lives are more important to us than our real lives, it can cause problems. We become obsessive about the number of likes we have, and our self-worth is measured by the number of friends or followers we have compared to others. We can easily forget about the people we share our real world with and stop communicating with them in exchange for what may be meaningless communication with complete strangers. Our marriage and relationships can suffer as we fall out of sync with our loved ones while we stay in touch with our virtual reality, scanning profiles and accepting friend requests at all hours of the day and night. For the compulsive, Facebook time eats into social time, family time, study time, work time, sleep time, exercise time, and dare I say it... our quiet time.

I put my hand up here. I have a Facebook page and a Twitter account as well as email. I try to spend the first part of my day with God, reading his word and talking to him about the day. A few years ago I started to read my Bible with an online study app, sent to me overnight by email. It means I go to my email account before I open my Bible, and often I feel a strong temptation to answer an email or reply to a message before I read that day's Bible passage. I always regret it if I do. At best I am distracted; at worst, I run out of time and don't get to start my day as I wanted to, with Christ.

I would also say that sometimes when I am reading or praying, the Lord might lay on my heart a particular word of encouragement for someone, or prompt me to ask someone for forgiveness. Having access to text messages and emails can be a really good thing because it allows us to communicate instantly. It's the repetitive, compulsive use of social media to the detriment of reality that causes a problem.

I have heard about "Facebook Families", where parents communicate with their children via social media. They might send them a message rather than walk into the next room. They might engage in their children's online conversations as though they were one of their teenage friends. And children refuse to answer phone calls from parents, telling them to communicate by social media. I am a little envious of tech savvy parents, but I have concerns when Dad or Mum acts more like a pal than a parent. If we allow social media to take over, it can be tempting to catch up on our messages rather than sleep. Studies suggest that a lack of sleep, particularly in teenagers, can lead to mental health issues. Even the devices we use, if not properly closed down, can emit light that reduces the quality of our sleep.

If we communicate exclusively online, we lose that level of intimacy that we need as human beings to function effectively. There may be a temptation to portray ourselves slightly differently than we are able to when we make new friends face to face. It may even be that we form relationships on false pretences, having lied about how we look or what our interests are, in order to be liked, or because we want to convey a certain image. Virtual socializing means we can hide behind more masks.

As with anything, we can develop compulsive and unhealthy behaviour patterns around our use of social media that drag us down and spoil our lives and our relationships. It's about finding balance, about us controlling our actions, not our actions controlling us. Are you concerned about the amount of time you spend on social media? Do you use it as a place to escape? Is it causing arguments or making you feel down? Take a break and set some limits. If you can't keep to these limits, it might be time to talk to someone.

A very wise person said to me, "If you were marooned on a desert island and you could choose one thing to have with you, what would that be?" The answer to that question, if you are honest and take some time to think about it, will give you insight into your priorities. The American pastor Louie Giglio explains how we can check our priorities:

How do you know what you worship? It's easy; you simply follow the trail of your time, your affection, your money and your allegiance. At the end of the trail you'll find a throne and whatever or whoever is on that throne is what's of highest value to you. On that throne is what you worship.

Review

Social media has revolutionized the way we communicate and has many benefits for society. But for some, it can become a compulsion that damages relationships and robs us of our freedom. If you have concerns about misuse, or overuse, take them seriously. It can be treated like any other compulsion.

Exercise

Remember that your use of social media has many advantages. But answer these questions truthfully:

- How much time do you spend on social media each day?

- Is the time you are spending on social media increasing?

- Do you ever open more than one Facebook window at the same time?

- Have you ever felt anxiety or distress as a result of your social media activity?

- Do you feel the need to talk about Facebook all the time, or do you worry about what has been posted on your wall in your absence?

- Do you ever substitute exercise, reading, or other activities you used to enjoy with Facebook? Do you use social media in the bedroom rather than interact with your spouse?

- Have you ever replaced going out for coffee with a friend for a Facebook chat, or messaged someone, or arranged a "virtual date" rather than meeting them and talking face to face?

- Do you have fake friends on your Facebook page? If 80 per cent of your friends are complete strangers, why are you befriending them?

- Have you ever been late for an appointment or missed a family mealtime because of your social media activity?

- Do you feel "high" or get excited when you see a post on your wall, when one of your messages is retweeted, or when you are tagged in a photograph?

  If answering these questions makes you feel uneasy, take a break, set yourself limits. If you can't keep to them, talk to someone about it.

CHAPTER 21

Recovery Partner

I was still in shock on the wet November evening when I first walked into a Gamblers Anonymous meeting. It was the day after my life had come crashing down. I don't think I would have had the courage to go on my own, but my brother took me and waited while I sat in a circle with twenty other guys. I was a little daunted and reluctant to share my story with strangers. What would they think? Would they judge me? I thought I had been able to hide until, just fifteen minutes before the end of the meeting, someone shared their story about how his wife had left him because of his gambling and had taken their son with her. He now had to watch as she formed another relationship, and her new boyfriend moved in and became his son's dad for most of the time. He cried as he told his story. I cried; most of us cried. And then the group asked me to share my story. I don't remember what I said, but I do remember the feeling of being in a place where people understood me, didn't judge me or try to fix me. They just knew what I was going through, and the feeling of empathy and camaraderie really helped me.

I had been walking through life on my own, isolated by my addiction, pushing away anyone who wanted to help, unable to love or be loved. But now I realized I was not alone. Addiction demands instant gratification. Recovery recognizes that it might take time. Addiction is lonely and self-centred. Recovery is a journey best followed in company, thinking of the needs of others as well as our own.

In chapter 12, on step 12, we discussed the benefits of helping

181

others on their recovery journey. Becoming a recovery partner, or sponsor as they are often referred to in the Anonymous fellowships, has benefits for both the sponsor and the sponsored. It is when we reach out to help others that we truly feel freedom from our addiction. If you are just setting out on your journey, try to find someone who is further along the track and ask them if they would consider walking with you for a while, just until you are over the great mountain you see blocking your way. They know you can make it through because they have walked that same path. You can take hope from the fact that if they can do it, so can you.

Recovery is not something you can read about and become free. There is no exam to pass or course to attend that will give you automatic recovery. It is not simple or instant, although I do believe in the power of Christ to heal and mend us. Often he does so through the intervention of someone who is able to take another by the hand and help to pull them up. This is why people almost always make better progress in a supportive recovery group or with another person than they do on their own. Sponsorship is a rewarding two-way street, and it has benefits for both.

The sponsored person benefits from:

- the certainty of knowing they are not alone, that at least someone understands and cares
- the hope that interacting with someone who has found recovery brings
- the knowledge and help of someone who has been through the challenge that they are facing
- having access to someone to share doubts, ask questions, and share problems with
- having someone to turn to when slips and relapses occur, who can encourage them and lift them up if they fall, or just help them when they feel tempted
- a pathway to further help if it is needed, and access to others in recovery.

The sponsor benefits from:

- enhancing their own recovery: by helping others they help themselves. Sharing makes it easier to live without our own addiction
- the satisfaction of assuming responsibility for someone other than ourselves for a change!

I have the privilege of sharing my recovery journey with others. It is a responsibility, it can be time consuming, and sometimes there are no answers, times when all we can do is provide a sympathetic ear. But the rewards are immense. For me, helping others whenever and however I can, within my schedule and my priorities, maintains my own desire to remain clean and healthy. As a sponsor, or just someone who wants to help a fellow human being, you will also experience that feeling of satisfaction. If you are in recovery and you find a sponsor, you have someone to share your burden, someone to encourage you and help you every step of the way, day after day.

There is a range of issues around sponsorship, such as: What makes a good sponsor? How do I find one? How do I know they can help? And there are responsibilities and conventions. There are no specific rules, other than the ones you set with your sponsor, but if this is an area you want to know more about, I would encourage you to read the Alcoholics Anonymous Questions & Answers On Sponsorship.

Just one word of caution. As addicts, there is a risk that we might be attracted to the concept of focusing on the addictive behaviour of others to the detriment of other, more important calls on our time. Our families and our work need to take priority or we will end up causing chaos in our lives while we try, well-meaningly, to prevent it in others.

Review

Becoming a recovery partner, or sponsor, is a huge responsibility, but it is also rewarding and satisfying. For an addict, finding and working with a sponsor could be one of the most significant things you do to achieve your recovery.

Exercise

- If you are in recovery, or want to start, find a recovery partner you can work with who has experienced the issues you are struggling with and come through the other side.

- If you can't find someone who has experienced your addiction, or even any addiction, an accountability partner is still worth finding. Recovery is most effective in community.

- If you have found recovery yourself, consider helping out at a local recovery group.

CHAPTER 22

Practical Advice

"Seek the Kingdom of God above all else, and live righteously, and he will give you everything you need."

Matthew 6:33

Do you ever feel as though you are drowning? That life is crushing you and you have lost control? All your plans and the projects you started are driving you, rather than you driving them. I felt like that a few months ago. I felt I was going through the motions. In my busyness to do stuff, I forgot the true reason why I was doing them.

I find it hard to say no to people; I don't like to let anyone down. In Christian ministry it is hard to say no without feeling guilty. We can accuse ourselves of being lazy servants and think rest is for heaven, so while we are down here we just have to do everything we can if it has any spiritual connection. I felt washed out, like I just didn't have anything left to give.

So I found a low-cost flight and booked myself a seat to my favourite place, the island of Jersey. I arrived with just an overnight bag, my Bible, and a notebook. It was early autumn. The season had been unusually dry and now the trees which lined the coastal path were on fire with an intensity of colour, carpeted by purple heather.

I wanted to find somewhere sheltered with a spectacular view. It didn't take long, and now, as I gazed out across a turquoise sea, I opened up my Bible. I was excited, expectant. I had a whole day just to soak up some wisdom. I felt sure God would speak to me through a dramatic verse and encourage and invigorate me, recommission me and restore my enthusiasm. I opened my Bible to the book of Isaiah, assuming God would speak through the powerful verses.

As time passed, instead of being inspired, I found myself distracted by the view, and by the sound of the circling seagulls overhead. I realized I hadn't brought anything to eat or drink. I began to think about food. I persisted with my Bible study, forcing myself to read. I expected a verse or a passage to stand out, but I felt nothing. Just an emptiness in my stomach. By early afternoon, I lost any hope that my "mini retreat" would lead to a dramatic new commissioning. I packed everything away and followed the coastal path, feeling a sense of disappointment.

It was a clear day, and as I walked I felt my spirits lift. It wasn't a school holiday or a weekend, so I had the path to myself. I felt like I wanted to sing, and immediately a verse came to mind. It was one I knew off by heart; it was so familiar to me I would probably have skipped over it had I been reading it. It was a verse that I used to sing when I was a young boy, in a round where the girls sang the verse then a chorus of hallelujahs while the boys sang the verse a second time. So it went, round and round, first in my head and then out loud. I just kept hearing it over and over:

Seek ye first the Kingdom of God,
and his righteousness,
and all these things shall be added unto you.
Hallelu, hallelujah.

All of a sudden I knew that those simple words, words I had learnt as a young boy and which were first spoken by Jesus in his Sermon on the Mount, were all the wisdom I needed. Sometimes we are so busy *doing* for God, we stop *living* for God. All he really wants from us is our love, our time, our loyalty. If we love someone, we want to please them. Living righteously brings pleasure to God. It also brings us peace and everything else we need.

This is my first practical tip: get your priorities right. Get them in order and everything else will follow. Suddenly, making decisions, which can seem so hard, becomes simple when we know what needs to come first.

In this chapter, I share some practical tips that might help you in your recovery. Apologies if they seem obvious. They are just things I have learnt, often the hard way, and have helped me:

- Priorities. Put God first in all you do.
- Live in the light. Don't have any secrets; don't do anything on your own that you would be ashamed to do in public.
- Make your quiet time a daily habit. Make sure it is a "quiet" time.
- Protect your spiritual health. This is precious. Ask yourself, is this activity good for my spiritual health or could it harm it?
- Be accountable to someone: a friend or your spouse, someone you respect and can be honest with. Meet regularly with them and give them access to the parts of your life you may try to hide.
- Have a sense of humour and be holy in your private life. Integrity shines out. My soldiers used to tell me they knew which officers would look out for them, those who were genuine, and those who just put on a show. Private holiness translates into public authenticity. Holiness and humour are so important. Holiness is not an optional extra; it is not just for saints and special Christians. It should be something we all aspire to in this life. It is a gift of the Holy Spirit, so be asking for more of it as well as striving to achieve it. The ability to laugh at ourselves is one of the keys to holiness because, when we don't take ourselves too seriously, it keeps us humble. Humility and holiness are closely linked, and humour is the bridge between them. I don't mean the kind of boring, pious, "I'm better than you" holiness. I mean the kind that C. S. Lewis wrote about when he said, "How little people know who think that holiness is dull. When one meets the real thing... it is *irresistible*."
- Ask for wisdom. Addiction is about instant gratification. When we apply wisdom to a situation, we have perspective. We make

the right decisions based on the long term, so we can look back on the decisions with a sense that what we did was right. "If you need wisdom, ask our generous God, and he will give it to you. He will not rebuke you for asking" (James 1:5). I ask for wisdom every day because I know I need lots of it. I know it's silly, but I still get surprised when I am able to view a difficult situation with clarity after I have prayed for wisdom. Some of the decisions I made as an addict were totally illogical, bordering on the insane. With wisdom comes perspective. If we can see things, situations, people, as God sees them, that for me is the ultimate wisdom.

- Understand your triggers. Look for patterns in your moments of weakness, your vulnerability, feelings and emotions, places, times, situations. For me, as I have said, thinking of HHALT helps – I am vulnerable to attack when I am hungry, happy, angry, lonely, or tired.

- Use blocks that work with your understanding of your triggers. Take drastic action if need be, such as moving home, finding a new job or new friends, avoiding situations that are dangerous, as well as doing simple things like taking a different journey home so you don't pass your local pub or bookie. Don't carry cash; download browser protection; give someone access to your accounts.

- Eat healthily, take walks, drink plenty of water, and respect yourself. Regular physical exercise will help increase your self-esteem. We have to be careful here, though, that we don't exchange one addiction for another, by allowing our pursuit of health or fitness to become compulsive so we end up worshipping our own bodies. The apostle Peter warns against this:

> Don't be concerned about the outward beauty of fancy hairstyles, expensive jewelry, or beautiful clothes. You should clothe yourselves instead with the beauty that comes from within, the unfading beauty of a gentle and quiet spirit, which is so precious to God.
>
> **1 Peter 3:3–4**

- Our young people today are under more pressure than ever to conform to continually increasing expectations of body shape. There is a huge rise in the number of young men taking and becoming addicted to substances that enhance their performance so they can spend longer in the gym. Often these substances are bought illegally, and they can cause harm. Social media can provide a forum for open discussion about how people look in a way we just would not do in open conversation.
- Make a budget and stick to it. If your compulsion has a financial aspect, your finances will be suffering and it is possible you may fall into debt. Debt is very destructive and drains us of self-esteem, motivation, and hope. If you are in debt, deal with it, face up to it. Seek help. Some creditors employ bullying tactics to frighten debtors into paying. A debt advisor will be able to help you. They helped me and gave me hope.
- Remember that your compulsion may have been your coping mechanism, your protection against the world. So when you choose recovery, you will have some short-term pain as you come face to face, often for the first time, with the issue you have been running from and will realize that your compulsion has only made it worse. Keep looking up. It's time to let Christ in and heal you from within.
- Pride will block recovery because it says, "I can do it on my own." The opposite of pride is humility. I constantly need to humble myself before Christ and remember I am here through his grace alone. It was pride that caused me to stop living in the light, pride in my own achievements. Then it was pride that stopped me asking for the help I so clearly needed.
- If you have found recovery, you will feel better, stronger, more in control. It's then that you will hear the voice saying you are no longer an addict, that you can cope now. Just one drink won't hurt. This is a form of denial and will lead to ruin.

PART 4

BEWARE

CHAPTER 23

Beware of Secrets

When we indulge our habits in secret, we often don't see the dangers. Neither can anyone else, so the only warnings come from ourselves. Behaviour patterns that may once have felt extreme to us become normalized over time. When we pull down the shutters, we suppress our consciences. The feeling that what we are doing is wrong becomes a feeling that what we are doing is normal. The voice we hear says, "It's OK, you're not hurting anyone. No one will know; it's not a problem." Or maybe, "Just this one last time, then I'll stop." These lies sound so much more plausible when we are the only ones listening. We do things unseen that we would never consider doing openly, and yet we never stop to ask ourselves why.

When we start to have secrets from others, we fabricate to maintain the secret, or we risk being found out. When people get too close – and it's generally the ones we love – we push them away and lie to them. We justify our lies by saying, "We are just protecting them; they don't need to know," or, "If they found out, it would hurt them." What we mean is, "If they found out, I wouldn't get away with it any more," or, "I would lose their love."

Secrets cause stress and conflict. They lead to lies. Honesty and openness is always the best path. It's not just the lies we tell others; we also become great at lying to ourselves, and the biggest lie of all is to tell yourself, "I do not have a problem."

Paul offers this advice to the Ephesians:

No more lies, no more pretense. Tell your neighbor the truth. In Christ's body we're all connected to each other, after all. When you lie to others, you end up lying to yourself.

Ephesians 4:25 (MSG)

Beware of the unseen

Understanding that the danger is not always obvious will help you to be on your guard. We use because it's generally pleasurable. The things we use might look harmless; they may be things everyone uses. Using can look quite attractive, on the outside. Gambling adverts make my blood boil because of the implications of fun, socializing, and winning. I have even seen one that implies betting is a way to get out of debt! The reality for me was misery, isolation, and loss. But we don't see the danger when everyone around us looks like they are having fun.

Just before my Channel swim attempt was due to take place, we all went to Devon for a family holiday. We were staying in an apartment complex right on the seafront. The boys couldn't wait for the tide to go out each day so they could search for crabs and shrimps in the many rock pools. I loved watching them with their buckets and fishing nets, clambering over the very same rocks I had clambered over as a child.

However, on that particular holiday, I preferred it when the tide was in, because it meant I could slip into the water and swim around the bay in preparation for my Channel challenge that was just a few weeks away.

I nearly made a huge mistake, one that could have had significant consequences for my health. I got the tides mixed up. The sea looked so inviting that late afternoon. The tide looked to be full and the water looked so inviting as it reflected the late afternoon sun. I could almost hear it calling to me. Although there was a bit of a swell, the waves weren't cresting. Each day that week I had swum for anything between an hour and three hours early in the morning, so I could have a full day with the family, but on this day Matthew had woken early and I'd missed my usual slot. I'd been feeling guilty all day about not swimming, and I wanted to get a swim in before it got dark.

As usual, I told Emma where I was going. I took my usual route out to deep water, following a small sandy gap in the rocks to a big tall rock with a hole that gave the village of Thurlestone its name. The rock stood alone, surrounded by sea, although you could walk out to it when the tide was low.

All seemed fine as I swam out to sea. I even had time to enjoy the relative cool of the water and the sensation of speed and rhythm. After about twenty minutes of swimming in the deep water, I began to notice the swell had increased and it was now quite choppy. I felt I should head back and be home in time for the boys' tea. But as I headed back towards the shore, I became aware of quite a strong current, pulling me out to sea. That in itself was not a problem. I knew the currents on this part of the coast were never stronger than my slow but powerful stroke.

That was when I saw the first luminous, long-tentacled jellyfish, just below the surface. They came in all shapes and sizes, large and small, and the whole range of colours, including the small blue variety that I knew were the most painful. I didn't mind the larger ones, those that were the size of a small dog; it was the fist-sized ones with longer dangling tentacles I wanted most to avoid. But when you hit a great cloud of them, they don't give you much room to take evasive action. And much worse was ahead.

I had been giving my full attention to avoiding a nasty sting, so by the time I looked up I was shocked to see I was quite off course. My sandy channel that I usually followed into the shore was way off to my right, and I knew I was now right over the top of a series of sharp, barnacle-encrusted rocks. The tide was going out fast, leaving the depth of water between me and their spiny pinnacles dangerously shallow. The swell meant that I was fine at the crest of each wave, but then the waves dropped me dangerously towards the hidden rocks. I feared that my ribs or my head would be crushed, but there was nothing I could do now except hope and pray.

What had looked like perfect, inviting conditions were in fact lethal. The golden surface of the water concealed the danger lurking below.

However inviting that cool glass of wine may look, however "fun" a simple bet is made out to be, what looks so harmless can be fatal if it is allowed to become part of a pattern of increasing misuse. If we go on relying on it to medicate our emotions, it can be just as dangerous to our health, both physical and mental, as those jagged rocks could have been to me that day.

When I finally made it to the shore, I made a mental note not to start my swim as the tide was turning. I got my head around the risks. Danger may not be obvious, but what appears to be quite harmless at first may become a slippery slope to disaster. C.S. Lewis wrote, "The safest road to hell is the gradual one – the gentle slope, soft underfoot, without sudden turnings, without milestones, without signposts."

Beware of denial

Whatever is denied cannot be healed.

Brennan Manning

Earlier this year I took delivery of a brand new car. It wasn't a Porsche; neither was it a kit car that looks good on the outside. I spend a lot of time on the road now, so I chose something that has good fuel economy, has a big boot for the children's things, and is comfortable to drive. I don't actually own the car; I lease it each month. I used to care what people thought of me as I arrived at places, particularly if I was meeting people for the first time, people who might base their opinion of me on the car I drove. Shallow, I know, but that's how I was.

My car needs a service. I know that, not because I have driven 10,000 miles and the manual says it needs a service, but because little things have begun to go wrong. It ran out of washer fluid for the windscreen. The oil warning light came on and my tyres have lost pressure. My brilliant on-board computer warns me of these things, and my brain tells me I need to get the car to the garage before something more serious happens. On the other hand, I could just ignore these warnings. My car still starts in the morning and still gets me to the station. I could just pretend all is well. No one who sees me drive to the station would know anything was wrong with the car, or that it is overdue for a service. I could just carry on. Until the car breaks down, that is. Because it will if I keep ignoring the warnings.

This is the first type of denial: knowing I have a problem, but no one else does, so I just ignore it and pretend all is fine.

If the car didn't have a sophisticated computer, I might not even know it needed more oil. I might not see the billowing smoke coming out of the exhaust as I drive down the street. Those on the side of the road who have to suffer the fumes would know, but I might choose not to believe them if they told me I had a problem.

This is the second type of denial: refusing to admit what everyone else can see.

If I continue to deny my car has a problem, the car will, at some stage, break down, possibly with serious consequences. On our journeys, we need our cars to function well. And we need to function well, not just on one cylinder. We need to keep ourselves serviced and fuelled. That is, if we want to reach the finish line.

One thing is for sure: even if our car is fully serviced and working fine, we could all do with a tune-up from time to time. Our tyres might lose their alignment and it will extend their life if we get the tracking fixed. We may not be suffering the effects of a full-blown addiction; we may not be in the ditch already, but let's be honest, we all have secret habits that cause damage. We could benefit from a trip to the garage to let a mechanic shine a light over all our working parts.

Or we may be blowing thick smoke and be just about to run out of fuel. Our engine might be about to seize because we haven't put any oil in it for the last 20,000 miles. We could already be in the ditch.

If you are reading this now and you know your car has broken down, then you are in a great place because the tow truck is about to arrive and take you back to the garage. You have no problem with denial; you know you need fixing. The mechanic can do some work on the engine as well as fixing the bodywork.

Beware of the lies

If you listen to your addiction voice you will hear these lies:

"It's not a problem; I could stop any time. I enjoy it; it helps me relax and it does no harm to anyone else."

"What I do is just what everyone else does. It's normal."

"Others do it much more than me; I just do it socially."

"Talking about it makes it worse; let's not over-analyse it."

"If you didn't have a go at me for it, I wouldn't need it in the first place."

Your addiction voice tells you, "The car still works; no one knows there's a problem. Why tell them something that will cause them to worry?" There is a fear, too, that if you own up, people will see the real you. But the reality is that continuing to drive with a warning light will cause serious damage to your car. Denial creates isolation, and isolation means we can indulge our habit further, leading to loneliness.

Loneliness reduces our self-esteem. We are created to live in community. Low self-esteem increases our craving to indulge our secret habits, and this increases our separation from God. In order to protect ourselves from the shame of contempt from others, we end up becoming cut off from those we love, to minimize the rejection we convince ourselves will result if we admit we have a problem. The cost, so often, is the loss of our most precious relationships with those closest to us.

I hid my habit from my wife for three years. Before that we had no secrets. I hid my habit because I was denying that I had a problem. When I knew I was in a bad way, my pride took over and stopped me being honest. It said, "You caused this problem; you are the only one who can fix it," and, "If I tell her she won't understand; she'll think it's something serious."

I love the way Paul refers to the connections between us. Denial isolates and disconnects. It also prevents us from finding the freedom Christ wants us to experience, freedom to choose what not to do as well as freedom to do things. The apostle Peter sums it up perfectly: "They promise freedom, but they themselves are slaves of sin and corruption. For you are a slave to whatever controls you" (2 Peter 2:19).

I have never been a very good liar. That meant, as my life became an increasingly complex web of deceit, I had to really concentrate on what I had lied about to follow through with my lies. I found myself writing down lies so I could refer to them if quizzed at a later stage. Long after Emma was asleep, I would still be awake, worrying about what would happen if she discovered my deceit. Denial increases the stress and worry caused by dishonesty. Our fears restrict our actions and our feelings. Worry is harmful and increases our craving to reach for the hand of our habit. We might find temporary relief, but when we wake up in the morning, the problems we cause by denial are still there.

Don't listen to the lies. Take that step out of the darkness of denial today and move into the glorious light of God's presence. During my years of addiction, I took a thousand steps away from my God. But by his grace, I only ever had to take one step back to him. He is waiting for you today.

Beware of fear

God is our refuge and strength,
always ready to help in times of trouble.

Psalm 46:1

I watched a film called *After Earth*. It's a great "father and son" movie set a thousand years after the earth had to be abandoned because humanity had mismanaged the ecosystem.

A legendary soldier and his son (played by Will Smith and his real-life son Jaden Smith) return to earth unexpectedly when their spaceship crashes. Will Smith is seriously injured and incapacitated, and his 13-year-old son is the only person left who can travel the 100 kilometres to set off a beacon that will enable their rescue.

Although desperate to be the son he thinks his father wants him to be, the son is crippled by anxiety and must confront a whole range of challenges before the ultimate battle against a highly evolved monster that feeds on human fear. The only way it can be overcome is by an attacker who has no fear and so is invisible to the beast. The boy's father remotely watches his son's progress and is able to warn him of danger and navigate for him by continually telling him that to give in to fear is a choice. When the boy gets scared and panics, his father calmly tells him to kneel. As the boy kneels in complete supplication, his father gives him the instructions he needs to keep going. I particularly love the part where the boy is saved from certain death as he finds himself in the open at night and exposed to freezing temperatures. As hypothermia begins to take hold, a huge bird drags him to shelter and then spends the night covering him with her wings. In the morning, the boy wakes up warm, but discovers the bird gave her life to save him.

It reminded me of Psalm 91:4: "He will cover you with his feathers. He will shelter you with his wings. His faithful promises are your armor and protection."

Inevitably, all contact with the father is lost and the boy must confront the beast on his own. He does so, and overcomes his fear, which, we discover, stems from a traumatic childhood event. The boy saves his father and they all live happily ever after.

"Get down on your knees before the Master; it's the way you'll get on your feet" (James 4:10, MSG). We need to "take a knee" and ask for reinforcements from God while saying no to the devil.

This film conjures many analogies in my mind in relation to fear. Fear blocks recovery.

Fear may well be the most basic of human instincts. Anyone who picks up a copy of the Bible will see time and again how God seeks to reassure us. I have different places I like to go to in God's word when I feel certain emotions, often to the psalms. When I feel in need of forgiveness I turn to Psalm 51. When I am scared, I find comfort in the psalms; there is something so genuine about the mighty warrior David when he cries out to God. He frequently faced down death in battle, and even his own family tried to kill him at one point. Psalm 46:2 reminds us, "So we will not fear when earthquakes come and the mountains crumble into the sea." But probably the greatest comfort to me is in the words he wrote in verse 4 of Psalm 23:

Even when I walk
through the darkest valley,
I will not be afraid,
for you are close beside me.
Your rod and your staff
protect and comfort me.

I hold on to these words very tightly because, even though I have knowingly walked through a minefield, jumped out of an aeroplane at 250 feet, been mortared, survived a helicopter crash, swum through the two busiest shipping lanes in the world, and patrolled streets where I knew I was a target for sniper fire, I sometimes feel quite scared.

I'm scared every time I wave goodbye to my boys at the end of a weekend, that they'll forget I'm their father and someone else will become dad in my place. Sometimes I'm scared I will be alone when I am old because the damage I caused was too much for my wife to stand by me. It's then that I need to take a knee and accept the certainty of the truth that I am loved, and I always will be, by my perfect Abba Father. Fear is something God can help me with; self-pity is something I can chuck over my start line.

There is a whole range of fears that block and prevent our recovery or drag us back over our start lines. We can even fear something that doesn't exist – fear of the unknown. We have a fear of what it will be like to permanently let go of the habit we use to medicate our fear! We fear the loss of control. We fear what others may think of us if we ask for help, which leads to denial. We fear finally having to confront resentments and pain. We fear failure, so we don't try. Above all we fear change and uncertainty. Richard Rohr talks about the ego in the same way as Brennan Manning talks about the "imposter":

> *What the ego hates more than anything else in the world is to change – even when the present situation is not working or is horrible. Instead, we do more and more of what does not work, as many others have rightly said about addicts, and, I would say, about all of us. The reason we do anything one more time is because the last time did not really satisfy us deeply.*[10]

According to W. H. Auden:

> *We would rather be ruined than changed. We would rather die in our dread than climb the cross of the present and let our illusion die.*[11]

I believe it's the fear of changing rather than the change itself that makes us so uncomfortable. Fear is often associated with loss of control.

---

10   Richard Rohr, *Breathing Underwater* (1989).
11   W. H. Auden, *The Age of Anxiety: A Baroque Eclogue* (1947).

My fears of not being loved or accepted drove me forward, but at what cost? When I speak to people with issues around eating, they often tell me that their choice of food is one way they feel they can take back control of a situation they have lost control of, and very often it's when they feel lonely. Food becomes a source of comfort, and something over which they can exert control. Sadly, the feeling it gives them doesn't last, it lowers their self-esteem, and in the end they lose control of when and what they eat.

When we feel fear we have a choice. We can either run from it by medicating – drinking, overeating, gambling, or taking drugs – or we can face down our fear and ask for a bit of bravery. Sometimes, when I get back to an empty house after dropping my boys back at the end of a weekend, I reach for my sword (the Bible, not my metal one!). Here are two verses that help me when I feel scared. One of them was written by a champion swordsman, and the verses swipe away my fear as good as any parry or upper cut:

> The Lord is my light and my salvation –
> so why should I be afraid?
> The Lord is my fortress, protecting me from danger,
> so why should I tremble?"

Psalm 27:1

The other verse is in a letter from Paul to his young protégé, Timothy:

> For God has not given us a spirit of fear and timidity, but of power, love, and self-discipline.

2 Timothy 1:7

When I read these verses, they don't instantly make me fearless, but they give me the strength to confront my fear and have some self-discipline. You can use the sword of the Spirit like that, too. It's how Jesus used God's words when he was tempted in the desert.

Some fears are not real; they're in our mind, like the monster under the bed. Such fears are easier to overcome than the fear of something real. We don't have to fear what *might* happen, and it should be our choice not to. Psalm 112:7–8 points the way:

They do not fear bad news;
they confidently trust the Lord to care for them.
They are confident and fearless
and can face their foes triumphantly.

Other fears are very real and very painful. Fear that arises from physical events needs care and love and proper unpacking in a safe environment. So many people are too fearful even to face their fears so they never seek the help of a professional counsellor. Again, the psalmist has some great advice: "But when I am afraid, I will put my trust in you" (Psalm 56:3).

Please don't let fear paralyse you, don't let it block your recovery, and don't let it drag you back over your start line. Ask God to shine his light on your fears and then give them to him. Get professional help if you need to, but don't suffer on your own in the valley of darkness. Remember that your gift is a spirit of power and self-discipline. Trust the promises God has made you through his word.

Beware of pride

Pride goes before destruction,
and haughtiness before a fall.

Proverbs 16:18

Pride prevents recovery because it tells us, "You can fix it. You got yourself into this hole; only you can get yourself out. No one else needs to know the truth."

As we have discussed, the opposite of pride is humility. We need humility for recovery, and we need it by the bucketful. Humility is a choice. We don't have to wallow in self-pity to be more humble. Humility, as C. S. Lewis points out, is "not thinking less of yourself; it is thinking of yourself less"[12].

Humility is something I can never have enough of. Pride was the single most destructive characteristic of my addiction. As I became more and more dependent on my gambling addiction, pride prevented me from seeking help. Pride made me pull down the blinds on my habit. Pride cut me off from my wife. Pride was what made me cover my tracks and lie to someone who didn't deserve to be lied to. Pride stopped me getting help. It stopped me from receiving God's grace. ("God opposes the proud, but gives grace to the humble", says 1 Peter 5:5.) My pride was only broken when I was completely humiliated.

I find it really satisfying to plant something and watch it grow, to feed it and water it, to protect it over the winter, and to be rewarded by a fruit or a beautiful flower. One of my favourite flowers is the clematis. It's a climber and also a good companion plant, so if you don't have a lot of space, you can brighten up a wall or a fence, a plain bush or a tree with some big, showy flowers. Clematis need a little care, though. They thrive in the sun as they grow, but the base of the plant should be shaded and never allowed to dry out. Otherwise they turn brown, wither, and die, almost overnight. Clematis also need pruning to grow the best flowers. There are lots of different kinds of clematis, but there are two main varieties, and they both need to be pruned very differently.

Early flowering clematis just need light pruning, a bit of tidying up. But late-flowering clematis need to be pruned back hard, almost to their roots, because all the flowers are generated on new stem growth. If you don't prune them back hard, they won't flower.

I was like a late-flowering clematis, and for three years I didn't produce a single flower. I needed to be brutally cut back in order for new growth to take place and for me to flower again. Sometimes in

---

12   C. S. Lewis, *Mere Christianity* (1952).

life we need to be cut back in order for us to produce fruit again, and it hurts. Oh boy, it hurts, but soon the pain is forgotten as we allow the gardener to create something beautiful.

Jesus said, "I am the true grapevine, and my Father is the gardener. He cuts off every branch of mine that doesn't produce fruit, and he prunes the branches that do bear fruit so they will produce even more. You have already been pruned and purified by the message I have given you. Remain in me, and I will remain in you. For a branch cannot produce fruit if it is severed from the vine, and you cannot be fruitful unless you remain in me" (John 15:1–4).

In the positive, he said, "Those who remain in me, and I in them, will produce much fruit." But he also gave us a warning: "For apart from me you can do nothing. Anyone who does not remain in me is thrown away like a useless branch and withers. Such branches are gathered into a pile to be burned" (verses 5–6).

How do we remain in him? Verse 3 shows us one way: Jesus said we have already been purified by his message, by the word of God.

On the day of my graduation from Sandhurst, I was given two very precious objects by two very special ladies. The first was my Sword of Honour, awarded to me by the Queen. The other was a small book, a devotional called *Living Light*. My mother gave it to me and in the front of the book she wrote me a note: "We realize that sometimes you will only have time for a few verses, so this might help. An army may march on its stomach, but spiritual food gets you even further."

I kept that little book and I read it every day, until one day when I thought I had made it, with my big salary and big job in the City of London. I stopped living in the light. When I read God's word, it's like a temperature gauge, an indicator of my spirit. If I am walking in the light, remaining in Christ, I listen to him through daily Bible study and meditation. If I am doing my own thing, my Bible and my *Living Light* will be collecting dust on the bedside table, or hidden away in a drawer. And my pride will block the intimacy of a healthy relationship with God. I'll be off doing something that will, in the end, lead to destruction. It's a pattern I can point to in my life. This message from Paul to the church at Corinth has helped me:

> *So to keep me from becoming proud, I was given a thorn in my flesh, a messenger from Satan to torment me and keep me from becoming proud.*
>
> *Three different times I begged the Lord to take it away. Each time he said, "My grace is all you need. My power works best in weakness." So now I am glad to boast about my weakness, so that the power of Christ can work through me. That's why I take pleasure in my weaknesses, and in the insults, hardships, persecutions, and troubles that I suffer for Christ. For when I am weak, then I am strong.*
>
> **2 Corinthians 12:7–10**

When we recognize our weaknesses and make ourselves vulnerable through our love for others and by being more humble, God's incredible power can shine through. All we have has been given to us by God, God who has placed us in the position we are in and God who made us who we are. When we accept that, there is no room for pride, arrogance, or self-satisfaction. Your abilities, gifts, and resources are all God-given.

I was worthless to God while I indulged my addiction, and even before that, puffed up as I was by my own achievements and successes, I wasn't bearing any fruit. Once the *Daily Mirror* article was published, the world saw me for what I was: fallen, flawed. And yet by pruning me back hard, the Gardener made my roots go down deeper. He got rid of my pride and made me realize I was not the person I had conned myself and others into thinking I was.

As someone who loves to potter around in the garden, this verse from Ephesians is underlined in my Bible several times. I love the translation in the Living Bible best:

> *And I pray that Christ will be more and more at home in your hearts, living within you as you trust in him. May your roots go down deep into the soil of God's marvelous love; and may you be able to feel and understand, as all God's children should, how long, how wide, how deep, and how high his love really is; and to experience this love for yourselves, though it is so great that you will never see the end of it or fully know or understand it. And so at last you will be filled up with God himself.*

Ephesians 3:17–19

I love the idea of pushing down my roots into the "soil of God's marvelous love". I know enough about gardening to understand that a good quality soil is the most important thing for healthy plants. Plants also need regular water, and sunlight. If we are too full of our own pride, our roots will be superficial and we won't truly be able to experience God's love and his gift of grace. Pride can have no place in my life. I need to put down my roots in God's love.

Beware of guilt and shame

I knew I had been forgiven. I could accept that Christ died for my sin. But I was finding it harder to accept that he chose not to even remember what I had done. I was finding it hard to forgive myself. Every day I felt the consequences of my sin. It was two months since I had prayed for forgiveness and healing. It was two months since I had last gambled. It was Christmas; I was alone and I felt the loss of my family. I felt guilty that my selfish actions meant my children would be waking up on Christmas Day and, for the first time in their lives, they wouldn't be opening their presents with their dad.

Guilt is different to self-pity. God can use guilt, when we feel convicted of our sin through our consciousness. However, still feeling guilty after we have confessed our sins and been forgiven is not healthy. My guilt pulled me down, made me feel unworthy of the gift of grace. It stopped me feeling loved by God.

My guilt was at its most intense in the weeks and months after I stopped gambling. I had to let go of it. I wish I could say it was easy to do. The truth is it was very hard, and I had to do it on a daily basis. Once I felt released from my guilt, it was all too easy for something to remind me of the pain I had caused. Emma found it very hard to forgive me. She wasn't doing it deliberately, but I could see the pain in her eyes and that made me feel guilty again. Each time I waved goodbye to Oscar and left him at the end of a weekend, I felt guilt for causing him pain.

I had to dump the guilt in the tip, leave it behind my start line, but I have been back to that start line several times with another car load of guilt to drop off. Guilt will both block recovery and can cause relapse.

Kevin was 28 and had been a gambler since the age of 14. He was desperate to get free from gambling. He had been attending Gamblers Anonymous meetings for almost ten years, on and off. His habit had caused the break-up of so many relationships. But he had been married to Shelly for two years now. They had a baby girl, whom Kevin loved dearly. He managed to keep his habit secret from his wife even when he lost his job as a plumber. He sold the tools his company owned for cash and lost the money at a high street bookmaker. His boss hadn't believed him when he said the tools had been stolen.

Kevin was a handsome guy and he had the gift of the gab. He could charm anyone. A few days after he lost his job, desperate for money, he called Shelly's elderly grandmother. She lived alone and he arranged to go and see her, but asked that she keep their meeting a secret from his wife.

When they met, Kevin broke down in tears and explained that all he had ever wanted was to buy his wife a little house so their daughter could grow up in their own home and not the council house they currently lived in. Kevin lied to the old lady: he told her he had a wage that would support a mortgage; he just didn't have the deposit the bank needed. He showed her a picture of a house he had picked up from an estate agent he had passed on his way to the meeting. His wife's grandmother was not a wealthy woman, but she had always saved up a little money for a rainy day. Now she thought she would be kind and give Kevin all her savings. She realized she was old and wanted to help her granddaughter and her charming husband. Kevin asked her if she would keep it a secret between them, and she agreed.

Kevin intended to use the £5,000 she had given him to pay off debts, buy back a ring belonging to Shelly, which he had secretly pawned, and clear the rent arrears on the house. But he calculated that £5,000 wasn't quite enough to clear everything, so he went to the bookmakers. At one stage he was £1,000 up, but he just kept putting the money back into the Fixed Odds Betting Terminal (FOBT). Over the course of five hours, he lost everything. He had wet himself because he didn't want to use the gents in the shop and risk losing his place on the FOBT. He couldn't bring himself to go home, so he walked the streets.

Three weeks later, his wife's grandmother suffered a stroke, and she died in hospital several days later. Before she died, she forgot her agreement with Kevin, and asked her granddaughter if they had moved in to their new house yet. Shelly confronted Kevin. She stood by him at first, but when her grandmother died, Shelly was unable even to look at Kevin without feeling a deep loathing, and kicked him out.

I met Kevin as he drifted in and out of Gamblers Anonymous (GA) meetings. He had moved back in with his parents and was trying to get free from his addiction. He would manage a few days, but every time he had any money he found himself back in the bookmakers. He told me that he just couldn't get the image of Shelly's grandmother out of his head. He was crippled with guilt, and the only way he could forget the image of her kind old face was to play roulette on the betting machines.

I had been invited to speak at a Celebrate Recovery meeting in Canterbury, and I invited Kevin. He wasn't a Christian, but he was desperate to try anything that might free him from his addiction and the guilt he felt. I picked him up in good time, and as we drove he really opened up. I had an opportunity to share my own story.

We never got to the meeting. There had been an accident and the emergency services closed the road while they carried out recovery. We were in the car together for five hours. Kevin became a Christian as we sat in the traffic jam. He wanted to be free from his guilt, and he accepted that Christ had died to take away our guilt and shame. I gave him my Bible.

I saw Kevin recently, and he has his smile back. His whole face looks different. For the first time in ten years, Kevin chaired a meeting at GA. He has been clean for five months.

As Joyce Meyer says, "Whatever your sin or failure, you need to confess it to God and then let it go. Stop punishing yourself for something that is in the past. Refuse to remember something God has chosen to forget."

Guilt is particularly dangerous when it's a by-product of addiction; the guilt we experience as a result of our addiction increases our desire to escape from it by using and, therefore induces a downward spiral of negative behaviour that is extremely hard to break. I call it the downward spiral of addiction: a chain of events that enslaves us while tricking us into believing the best way to escape is to keep using.

If we accept that we make a choice to carry guilt with us, then we should accept that we can let it go. We do this when we accept the gift of God's grace. We can't earn it. Isaiah is one of my favourite books in the Bible. A year ago I was reading a verse from Isaiah that felt very relevant to me and my life at that moment; it felt like God was addressing me personally. It made my skin tingle and I had to get out of bed and down on my knees, so real was the feeling that God had just spoken to me. Paul, in his second letter to Timothy, reminds him that "All scripture is God-breathed" (2 Timothy 3:16,

NIV UK). I felt as though God had just breathed those words.

Here are two verses from Isaiah that help us to deal with guilt. All we have to do is accept that they are true:

Come let us talk this over, says the Lord; no matter how deep the stain of your sins, I can take it out and make you as clean as freshly fallen snow. Even if you are stained as red as crimson, I can make you white as wool!

Isaiah 1:18 (Living Bible)

Let men cast off their wicked deeds; let them banish from their minds the very thought of doing wrong! Let them turn to the Lord that he may have mercy upon them, and to our God, for he will abundantly pardon!

Isaiah 55:7 (Living Bible)

Here in these verses are all the words we need to overcome our secret habits. These are verses to be treasured and learnt off by heart!

My grandfather was an evangelist. So many people came to hear him speak that they filled the Royal Albert Hall to overflowing on thirty consecutive Saturdays. He was a humble man who loved God, and he recognized the true value of the word of God, the sword of the Spirit. He memorized almost the entire New Testament; in fact, he reached the book of Revelation before he was suddenly taken home at the age of 56. My mother tells me stories about how he would go for a "Romans walk" and recite the whole book to himself as he walked.

I remember growing up in Sunday school and having to memorize verses. In the age of smartphones and tablets, perhaps we have lost the art of memorizing verses, even though we are told to store up his word in our heart (Psalm 119:11).

In the two verses from Isaiah, we see a recovery sequence laid out in order:

- We need to stop, to cast off our deeds, to physically abstain.
- We need to stop thinking about our habit: don't even entertain the thought.
- We need to turn to Christ and get intimate with our God.
- He will then forgive us. Every time he will abundantly pardon us.
- Repeat until we get it.

If he can abundantly pardon, who are we to challenge that with our human thoughts of, "I've gone and done it again. That's it now – I have no hope of being forgiven. He just can't keep on forgiving me time and time again." He can forgive and he does forgive, and when he does, he chooses to forget what we have done, and he makes us whiter than snow. The problem then lies within us and with the whispered words of the deceiver: we don't see ourselves as pure as freshly fallen snow. Especially when we are surrounded by people we have hurt and upset, and by situations where our habits have caused damage to relationships and trust that may never be fixed.

We have a choice here. We can keep going back to our habit to try to make ourselves feel better. Or we can choose to break the spiral of addiction, step over that line once and for all, and accept the truth that by God's abundant grace and the wonderful gift of Christ to us on the cross, we are forgiven and we are loved. Forgiveness and total, all-embracing, unconditional, unchanging love: these are God's gifts. He won't take them away. He doesn't love people because of what they do; he loves them despite what they do because we are his creation. If you can accept that truth, you will have freedom. I'm not saying you will never indulge your habit again, but if you can grasp that simple truth, you won't be a slave to your actions any more. You won't need to escape.

Guilt is a self-indulgence we recovering addicts cannot afford. Brennan Manning describes how a preoccupation with self is a component of unhealthy guilt:

It stirs our emotions, churning in self-destructive ways, closes us in upon the mighty citadel of self, leads to depression and despair and pre-empts the presence of a compassionate God. The language of unhealthy guilt is harsh. It is demanding, abusing, criticizing, rejecting, accusing, blaming, condemning, reproaching and scolding. It is one of impatience and chastisement. Christians are shocked and horrified because they have failed. Unhealthy guilt becomes bigger than life.[13]

We should not confuse guilt with our conscience, which, when fully functioning, is a useful instrument to assist us in choosing to do the right thing and recognizing what is wrong. Our consciences allow us to accept the gift of forgiveness. Unhealthy guilt becomes self-commendation which suppresses the helpful conscience and replaces it with a negative, paralysing gloom that does not allow us to accept the gift of God's grace.

John R. Claypool, in *Learning to Forgive Ourselves*, explains the importance of accepting God's grace:

The moment the focus of your life shifts from your badness to his goodness and the question becomes not "What have I done?" but "What can he do?", then release from remorse can happen; miracle of miracles, you can forgive yourself because you are forgiven, accept yourself because you are accepted, and begin to start building up the very places you once tore down. There is grace to help in every time of trouble. That grace is the secret to being able to forgive ourselves. Trust it.[14]

Beware of regrets

The year was 2011 and it should have been one of the happiest years of my life. Oscar had been born the year before without any

---

13   Brennan Manning, *The Ragamuffin Gospel* (1990)
14   James William Cox and Kenneth M. Cox (eds), *John R. Claypool Best Sermons 1* (1988).

complications and Matthew, now three, loved playing with him. We lived in the country and I had a working week that allowed me to work from home most of the time. It should have been a perfect family situation.

Emma was a natural mother and tried to create a routine that was comforting for Matthew, who had recently been diagnosed with autism, while providing security and familiarity for Oscar. She cooked tea for all of us at 5 p.m., the boys enjoyed an hour of play, and then they both had a bath, got ready for bed, and each had a story in their own bedrooms.

Just two years previously, my commute to London on the train meant I had to leave home before 5 a.m. and I was rarely home before 8 p.m., five days a week. Now I had the opportunity to engage with my children, to be a part of their routine, to read to them and kiss them goodnight.

"Do you want to give them a bath tonight?" Emma asked me, passing me the bowl of mashed potatoes. It must have been so hard for her to see me drifting in and out of my moods. I could be happy and engaging, playing trains and tunnels or planes and runways as I fed the boys their food, making them laugh with my silly animal noises and pulling faces at them. Or I could be completely distracted, alone in my troubled thoughts. It just depended on the success of my betting that afternoon. Often I wouldn't even come down and share in the meal.

"I can't. I have to take a call from the States," I lied.

"Oh pleeeaase, Daddy. You said you would this time." Matty always remembered any promise I ever made. He never forgot anything.

Behind the closed door of the spare room I used as my office, I could hear the laughter and splashing from the bathroom. Then the door opened and in rushed Matty and Oscar, their little bodies covered in bath foam. I quickly closed down the screen that had been streaming a live tennis match from some obscure part of the world. It was the deciding set and I was losing. I heard myself shout as they jumped on the bed. Matty stopped bouncing and pushed out his bottom lip. Oscar just ran for the safety of his mummy's arms.

"There's no need to shout like that; they just wanted to say hallo. Come on, Matty, let's get you dry."

Over the three years of my addiction, I lost the house I owned. I sold my car for a fraction of what it was worth, along with most of my possessions. I lost my job and my reputation in the City. I also squandered three-quarters of a million pounds, washed it down the drain. I sold my precious Sword of Honour and even my own wedding ring for cash.

Many of the things I threw away have been restored to me. I don't have any debts and my work is now fulfilling and rewarding. But for many months I laboured under the strain of regret. Every time I was blessed financially, I didn't see it as anything other than a hopeless drop in the ocean. It could never restore my fortunes, and whatever I earned, I just kept thinking it should have been on top of what I had had before.

One Sunday, after Emma came back with the boys and we made our home together in a rented cottage, we took the children to explore Tunbridge Wells. Tunbridge Wells is a spa town, and on Sundays, the crowds of busy shoppers are replaced by people with more time to just walk and enjoy the old streets.

I was playing a game with the boys which involved running between the pillars of a Victorian shopping arcade. I had once played the same game in the same place with my brothers and sisters. I looked back to see where Emma was. She was staring into the window of an estate agent.

As we drove home, she seemed unusually quiet. "The prices down here are much higher than in the north, aren't they?" She looked at me and I didn't know if she was asking me or telling me. "But we would still have been able to afford three bedrooms and a garden, if you hadn't wasted all our money," she said, as we drove past a beautiful Georgian terrace.

I felt all the regret and self-pity, the loathing and the gloom. I had destroyed my credit history, and with it any chance of getting a mortgage. It would take years to save for a deposit, in any case.

While Emma may have felt the financial loss, my biggest regret was for all the bathtimes I missed. All the storytimes, the chances to tuck the boys up in bed, the games of trains I left halfway through, and all the games of garages I turned my back on while I checked the progress of a bet I had placed. I even regret the nappies I didn't change.

Late last summer I went for a walk. The sun was shining through the leafy canopy, providing me with my very own light show. But I wasn't looking at the trees. My head was down and all I saw was the mud I was stepping in. I felt rather than heard the instruction to "look up". That was when I saw the beauty all around me. I realized I was holding on to regrets and they, in turn, were holding me back. I was living in the past. I couldn't go any further on my recovery journey until I stopped looking back, stopped regretting and imagining what the future would have been like if I hadn't self-destructed. I needed to be thankful for the here and now, to look around and enjoy the moment – this moment – and to let go.

Later I found my start line stone and I let go of my regret. I dumped it over the line. No amount of regretting would change my past, but by choosing not to regret, I had a chance to have a richer, better, and happier present.

One of the things that perpetuates the need for a gambler to keep gambling is the desire to chase the loss, to try to recover your money, or even recover winnings you later lost. You regret not cashing in when you had the chance, so you put even more money on an even more reckless bet to try to win back the money. Usually it leaves you in an even worse position.

I will never get back the time I lost with my children, but feeling down about that won't change it. However, I can control the quality of the time I can and do now spend with them. If I can take the negative emotion of regret and use it as motivation to try to be a better dad in the here and now, I know that, in a small way, my loss will not be wasted.

My actions didn't just affect me. Emma carried regrets too. We talked about it and I told her how it made me feel when she spoke about the regret she felt. I chose not to regret. I still choose not to regret, every day. But we need to accept that other people we have affected by our actions may also carry regrets, and we need to be sensitive to their feelings in the same way we would like them to be sensitive to ours.

Regret, like unhealthy guilt, is a negative and destructive emotion. Regret can also be a source of self-loathing, of disgust at our actions. Self-disgust is a huge threat to us as addicts. In our heads we understand we are inheritors, sons and daughters of the living God. But in our hearts we can't love ourselves or even feel comfortable in our own company. If we can't like ourselves, we can't accept the wonderful healing that comes with the certainty that we are loved unconditionally.

The pattern of the way we think about ourselves is often formed in early childhood by a remark made by another child, a teacher, or something our parents say. Mostly it is because we didn't feel sure of the love of both our parents. But one throwaway line may have a quite devastating and lifelong effect on our self-esteem, just like the comment to Sophie in the school changing room. Even the non-verbal messages we pick up as we are developing can have a huge influence over us. Things like, "We wanted a boy", "You were a mistake", or, "I wish you were more like your sister". Comments we don't really mean as parents can be taken to heart, such as, "You are good for nothing, you are so stupid, you'll never make it in life."

My editor encouraged me to imagine our childhood selves as being like a ball of clay that gets harder as we find our way in life. When we are young and the clay is soft, little things can still make a big impression. Those impressions can go deep and are not easily erased. Low self-esteem locks us into a pattern of escape where we end up doing harmful things that make us feel a little bit better for a very short time, before we end up feeling very bad about ourselves. We need to break this pattern by doing good things that make us feel better, both temporarily and long term. It can be small things like taking a walk, appreciating a view, great music, a good book, a taste, or just some time with a loved one. When we worship God, we forget ourselves and focus on him. In doing so, we end up feeling better about ourselves.

If you are a parent, be careful what you say. Those who hurt, hurt others. Maybe it's time to break the cycle.

PART 5

LIVING IN THE LIGHT

CHAPTER 24

The Light of the World

"Look! I stand at the door and knock. If you hear my voice and open the door, I will come in, and we will share a meal together as friends."

Revelation 3:20

My meeting in the financial district finished early. I looked at my watch. I had an hour before I needed to be at the station. I left the office and headed west. It hadn't rained for several weeks, but now big droplets began to splash on the hot pavement. I made good progress, despite the rain. The groups of tourists and schoolchildren all seemed to be heading the same way, hurrying to reach their next destination. I wanted to see a painting in St Paul's Cathedral. I'd waited all summer for the right opportunity.

My parents went to church every Sunday without fail, so I was a regular at Sunday school. I disliked anything with the word "school" in it, so I probably spent the whole time making the lives of all my Sunday school teachers a misery (and the rest of the week I did the same for all my school teachers).

But there is one Sunday I have never forgotten. I was probably no more than eight years old when my Sunday school teacher, Mrs P, brought in a picture. It had a gold frame, but it wasn't the frame that was remarkable. I just stared at the picture as Mrs P explained the symbolism the artist had incorporated into the most beautiful painting I had ever seen.

To understand the beauty of the picture that captured my imagination, you really need to see it for yourself. If you don't know

the picture, *The Light of The World* by William Holman Hunt, you can find it online. You may even have seen copies or prints. However, as I discovered on that late summer's day, to really experience the utter beauty and power of the picture that was inspired by Revelation 3:20, you have to see the original, life-size painting.

As my small briefcase was searched by a security guard, I asked where I could find the picture. When I saw it, it took my breath away. I felt an urge to kneel before the image of Christ. Other visitors must feel the same because prayer cushions are provided along a rail beneath the picture.

Kneeling and now looking up at the picture, I could see it in all its splendour. It wasn't the painting itself that made me "take a knee"; it was the face of Jesus, framed in a halo of light. It made me think of a scripture. I didn't know the verse by heart, but I knew where to find it. I borrowed a Bible from the back of a nearby chair which had been laid out for a service. I loved it that, although St Paul's Cathedral is a landmark, a tourist attraction, it is also very much a place of worship. A choir was rehearsing as I took the Bible back over to the painting and found the verse I was looking for.

You see, we don't go around preaching about ourselves. We preach that Jesus Christ is Lord, and we ourselves are your servants for Jesus' sake. For God who said, "Let there be light in the darkness," has made this light shine in our hearts so we could know the glory of God that is seen in the face of Jesus Christ.

2 Corinthians 4:5–6

As I gazed upon the face of Christ, I saw that light. The figure in the painting is standing in a dark wood. At his feet are the weeds and rotten apples that represent our sins. He is standing at a door and knocking, but he is facing away from the door, towards me, as though about to leave. For although he wants to open the door, which represents my and all of our hearts, he can't open it from the outside. The artist has not painted a handle. If Christ is to come into our lives and shine the lantern that casts such beautiful light in the darkness of the background, we have to let him in.

Freedom

I realized my cheeks were wet before I knew I had been crying tears of joy, tears of gratitude for my own gift of freedom. A freedom that was fully paid for in pain and ultimately death by this perfect, gentle man, the Son of God. All I could do was thank him for blowing away my dark clouds, for the gift of a new intimacy, the freedom to choose.

Life is not perfect. I live with the consequences of my sin. But I do so in the hope of a perfect life to come and the knowledge that he is walking with me every step of the way down here. We should never put people on a pedestal and see them as more spiritual, more recovered – God doesn't. We need to be set free so we can show the world what it is like to be "free indeed", full of the joy that comes from the certainty of knowing we are all sons and daughters of God and inheritors of the riches of eternal life. There simply is no room for a secret habit, and there should be no need to become enslaved.

It is easy to see ourselves as set up for a life of failure. God doesn't see us that way; he loves us. He made us as we are, and we are prone to falling. We need to remember to ask him for a hand when we do, and not try to be brave on our own or look for help elsewhere. I know I need to keep telling myself not to be so harsh. We should go easy on ourselves. We will slip, but it's a journey we will never complete until we leave this earth. That doesn't mean we are not loved or not good enough to be loved. We should live for the moment with no regret, not waiting for how it will be, but enjoying the present. We are forgiven by God's grace. He knew we would slip up. We can't afford to go through every day feeling that we have failed, and we don't need to, because his love is not held

back for the perfect. We can accept that we are not perfect and be happy that we are still loved.

By the time I left St Paul's Cathedral, the rain had stopped. Puffy white clouds scudded across the strips of sky between the towering buildings of the London skyline. I realized I was happier than I had ever been. Not because of anything I had done, but because I had come to realize I was loved. It was the end of the summer, and Emma had told me she was taking the boys and never coming back. I may have lost something that was very precious to me, but as I write these words I know I am going to drive up and spend the weekend with them in a few hours' time. I am content with what I have. I am genuine for the first time in my life. I am real, transparent, and feeling whole and honest. I don't feel I have to pretend any more. Life is a journey, so let Christ lead you. Don't be too harsh on yourself or overly critical: remember you are his creation, and above all, don't give up along the way when it gets hard.

Jude 24 says, "He is able to keep you from slipping and falling away, and to bring you, sinless and perfect, into his glorious presence with mighty shouts of everlasting joy. Amen" (Living Bible).

The only thing you have to do if you want to experience true recovery is to open the door of your heart to the one who stands and knocks. He's knocking now. You may have already opened it, but somehow your compulsion, your addiction, has allowed the door to swing shut again. Maybe you hadn't even realized. Open it up again and let his light shine in.

But now you are free from the power of sin and have become slaves of God. Now you do those things that lead to holiness and result in eternal life. For the wages of sin is death, but the free gift of God is eternal life through Christ Jesus our Lord.

Romans 6:22–23

CHAPTER 25

Journey's End

God will bring me out of my darkness into the light, and I will see his goodness.

Micah 7:9 (Living Bible)

I had been in the water for ten hours. I went through my mental checks. My shoulders were OK, although tired and a bit stiff. Actually, every time I took a stroke it hurt. It really hurt, an "ouch" hurt every time I pulled, but I didn't acknowledge the pain. It was manageable. My shoulders didn't feel heavy; I still had a few hours more if I really needed them. My tummy was OK too: no digestion problems; I hadn't felt the cramp I had been told to look out for when you drink a concentrated carbohydrate mix every hour. I didn't want to waste time taking on any solids. I had managed to keep my feed times down to just over a minute, treading water while I gulped down the warm liquid from the bottle thrown out to me on a line. Keeping the feed times short was essential if I wanted to avoid being taken hundreds of metres off course by the strong tidal current.

I didn't feel cold, but I acknowledged that the sun had been out all day; now the sun had set I could feel the air getting colder. It was getting dark now; I didn't want to swim in the dark. I hadn't trained in the darkness, and all the way through the day I had been able to swim in the lee of the boat, protected from the wind. I had listened to Stuart's advice and stayed as close to the boat as I could while he navigated safely through the shipping lanes, his GPS constantly tracking the risk of a collision with a supertanker. He

was broadcasting a coded radio signal, warning ships to keep away. I didn't know it at the time, but we had passed worryingly close to the biggest container ship in the Maersk Line fleet, a 1,306-foot supertanker.

As darkness approached I was feeling tired, but I was in good shape. I had no intention of giving up. My brother Richard was preaching that evening at my church and he pulled up a live feed GPS track of my swim on the overhead projector. It looked as though I was just about there and likely that I would make land at some point during the next hour. At home, Emma was also following the track of my swim.

Not wanting to swim in the dark, I put my head down and I gave it all I had, thinking I was almost there and assuming the worst must be behind me. But, as a swimmer, you don't really know very much other than the green water below you, the sky above you, and your support boat. Occasionally I saw a boat ahead or to my side. My observer, Phil, saw much more and made official notes he would later need to submit. If there was any medical emergency, those notes would be important. Phil saw a pod of dolphins swimming with me and a seal who kept me company for an hour. I wasn't aware of any wildlife except the jellyfish I desperately tried to avoid swimming through. I thought I knew what was ahead of me. Had I known even half of what lay ahead, I would not have felt so confident.

As I swam in close to the boat to get a feed, I wanted to ask if they could work out an estimated time of arrival, so I could pace myself. I remember Stuart, my skipper and pilot, telling me just to stay close to the boat now and go for it.

The next three hours were life-changing for me. I will share a few excerpts from the observer's log, starting around the time it began to get dark:

"19.30 hrs – Feed. Justyn asks, 'Does the skipper give ETAs?' 'No mate, the only person in charge of this swim is you. Now get back out there and start swimming for the coastline you can see in front of you. Justyn smiles, feeds, and swims, knowing that with every stroke he is getting closer to his dream."

Just before it got dark, I saw the French coast. It was just a dark shape in the fading light of my longest day. I saw a pinprick of light on the coast and I thought, "That's it. I've cracked it. I can do this." But something was confusing me: as I headed on towards France, the boat seemed to be going the wrong way. I just thought I didn't need them as much now, especially if they wanted me to go in a roundabout way.

I thought I knew best, but I was making a big mistake. Unlike my pilot, I had no idea what the current was trying to do to me. He was aiming off, setting the boat against the tide, trying to take me round the back of Cap Gris Nez, so when the tide turned it would bring me back to shore at a time when I most needed a helping hand.

That day, I later discovered, was a day when the tidal currents were at their most influential of the whole summer, a 6.5 m height was recorded, which meant I swam in a huge 'S' shape and covered a lot more distance than the 33 km straight line. No other swimmer that year had successfully crossed with such a strong tide. At the time when I most needed to stay close to the boat, I ignored the advice. But it was at that point that the wind started to pick up. I didn't realize it at the time, but the wind was blowing in the opposite direction to the force of the tide and was a fifteen-knot north-easterly. It had been gentle two-knot breeze when I had set off.

That meant one significant thing for me, and I was very much aware of it. The wind and the water in opposition meant waves. As it grew dark, I couldn't see the shape of the boat and it was much harder to line myself up alongside it. Anyway, I thought, the boat is going in the wrong direction. I tried not to remind myself that it was at this point in the swim last year and the year before that two swimmers had lost their lives. I kept turning my arms.

"20.10 hrs – Justyn has swum too far from the boat again. I stand on the back bench of the boat in moderate but increasing swell and shout for him to come back closer. He shouts back, rather frustrated, saying he is trying, but it's difficult to get his bearings. The wind has increased and the tide is running against the wind causing a difficult swell. Justyn is fighting through it."

I realized I had to concentrate more now it was dark, but I was cold and pushing close to exhaustion. In the light I could see when a wave was about to break over me. But in the darkness, as I turned my head for air, I frequently swallowed a mouthful of cold sea water. The salt burnt the back of my throat and I felt it closing up. I felt my tongue swell up. It was hard to get enough air. I felt like I was being thrown about and I couldn't find any rhythm. As I fought against the sea, the tide, and myself, I drifted further from the boat, still convinced all I had to do was head straight for the lights of the French coast.

"21.00 hrs – Feed. Justyn is still fighting across an ever-increasing tide. The wind has picked up even more now and it's a heavy swell. We are being dragged back past 'The Cap'. Justyn is told that from now on he will need to dig deeper and swim harder to battle across the tide to land. We are entering an area of water we have nicknamed 'The Washing Machine' because of the wind and tide working against each other and churning up the sea. This is going to be the toughest part of the swim. Come on, Justyn, you are almost there."

Back at church, Richard finished his sermon and flipped the overhead back to my track, assuming it would show I was home and dry. To his surprise, and the surprise of the 200 people who were worshipping that evening, my track showed I was further away than I had been at the start of the service. Something was wrong. They all began to pray.

"21.30 hrs – No feed given owing to the rough conditions and the speed of the tide. If we stop to feed now it could add another hour or more to Justyn's swim time and we are still in 'The Washing Machine'."

I knew something was very wrong. The lights I was heading

for were not getting any closer. In fact, the lights on the coast had disappeared. I could still make out the dark shape of the coast, but what I didn't realize was that because the tide was so strong that day, there had been no slack tide as the tide turned. Stuart's plan was to try to get me down past "The Cap" and then really push hard in the half-hour just before the tide turned. But there was no slack period. It went from fast in one direction to fast in the other. I had missed "The Cap" and now the tide was taking me up the coast towards Belgium. If I was going to make land in the next five hours I would have to punch through a very strong current.

I was in real trouble. So I did what I always do when I realize my frailty and weakness, when I acknowledge that a situation is beyond my own control: I prayed.

When I saw the light on the boat, I wondered what they were doing. I even thought they were fishing and remember how odd that seemed to me at the time. They kept calling me, but the boat was too far away now for me to hear anything clearly above the sound of the wind and the waves. And then I realized what they were doing: they were so concerned about the way I kept swimming off in the wrong direction, they shone a light on the water by the side of the boat where they wanted me to swim. They wanted me to swim in the light.

It had been my pride, my confidence in my own ability that kept taking me out into the darkness. I summoned all my strength and fought against the tide to swim back towards the boat. When I reached the patch of light I felt sheltered from the wind. They gave me a feed that tasted like treacle. Now, each time I turned my head, I could see when a wave was about to break. I stopped drinking salty sea water. I could hear Carolyn's words of encouragement. I felt power in my arms, not pain. I pulled harder.

"21.50 hrs – Justyn has battled hard through 'The Washing Machine' and has come out the other side. Still a strong tide, but the sea is now calmer so we stop for what we tell Justyn is his last feed. Unknown to Justyn we have concentrated his feed: three spoons of fruit sugar and double the dose of CNP [carbohydrate powder mixed with water and fruit cordial]. We tell him to use the last of his reserve and dig really deep now and make this the last leg. He smiled back at us and said 'OK'. Threw the feed bottle at me and set off swimming hard."

I had no idea how close or how far away I was; I just knew I had to punch through the tide or I would have to wait for the tide to turn. I knew I didn't have another five hours in my shoulders, so I went for it. I don't know where I found the strength, but I am sure it was a gift! Now I could see the coast much more clearly, and a bright light on top of the cliff illuminated a building of some sort. The light gave me my bearings. This time the boat and swimmer headed directly for the light. And then the *Sea Leopard* just stopped. I assumed the engine had failed and just thought, No, not now. I'm so close, please don't break down on me.

"21.56 hrs – Stuart has the Rib [a small inflatable boat used to accompany the swimmer to the coast when the sea is too shallow to allow the boat, *Sea Leopard*, to get any closer to the shore] in the water and is coming round *Sea Leopard* to begin to guide Justyn into shore. I shout to Justyn to tell him to follow the Rib, but he can't see it and shouts back, 'What do I swim for?' I look towards the coastline and see what I think is a church. It is so brightly lit it looks like it is on fire under orange lights. Rising from the back of the church is a spotlight going straight up into the cloud with a light haze around it. It is the brightest thing for miles around. I smile and shout back to Justyn, 'Can you see the church on land?' He confirms he can see it, and I tell him to head for that."

Now I can see this church with a tall steeple. It's the only light and the only building on the whole stretch of coast. As I leave the safety of the boat and strike for shore, I can feel the water is warmer and the sea has gone completely calm. I feel absolutely no pain in my arms. I feel like I could sprint and set a new 100 m record. The church looks as though it's on fire!

"Justyn sets off again and we follow his flashing swim lights as he begins to cross the bay heading for the illuminated church. Stuart tells me he has never seen that church before and that this stretch of coast is usually in total darkness. Tonight, though, Justyn has his marker to head for and he's making good progress. He is really close now. Keep it on Justyn, almost there.

"22.10 hrs – I see his swim lights rise up out of the water and then disappear as he turns round and faces the *Sea Leopard*. I can hear him, and we are informed over the radio from the Rib that he is clear of the water. He has done it. Great job, Justyn, you are now officially a Channel swimmer."

I have no words to express the feeling I had when I felt sand under my feet. I wanted to shout and cry at the same time. It felt like I was in a dream. I felt disconnected from my physical body. I looked up at the church and said a huge thank you to God, my rock. Then I turned and looked back out to sea. What I saw wasn't the Channel. I was looking back on the journey of my life. He has never failed me, and even though I think I know best sometimes, he is always there to guide me. He was my strength when I was weakest. He held me when I was in the darkest part of my life, battered by the waves I had created. He never stopped loving me and all my imperfections. I know with complete certainty that he will never abandon me. That knowledge liberates me to be myself. I don't need the superficial affirmation of others. I have no need or desire to escape from a reality that is secure and full of joy.

When I do my own thing, my life is a dark and lonely place. But when I submit my will to his care, I am surrounded by the light of his love and grace. I want you to stand in that light, to feel that love too, because that is where freedom can be found. It's a gift: take it, embrace it, enjoy it.

"22.20 hrs – A very happy and relieved Justyn is back on the *Sea Leopard* and we are beginning our journey home. I tell Justyn about the church and he asks if anyone has taken a picture. He sits on the engine box looking over the stern of the *Sea Leopard*, quietly contemplating what he has just done. He does not take his eyes off the church as it slowly begins to disappear in the night and we make our way home, across the sea."

One small journey came to an end. But my real journey has only just begun. When I was tested by the storms of life, I discovered my house was built upon sand, and it fell flat with a great big crash. I am a long way from perfect, but that recognition is now a strength as I recognize I need to build my foundation on the solid rock of Christ. I walk each day with him in charge, not me. I intend to live my life in the light. I'm not driving, so I'll just enjoy the view. I'll live in the here and now. One day at a time.

Postscript

My pilot and my observer were not Christians. But the sight of that church, lit up on top of the cliff, profoundly affected them. They had never seen it before in twenty-seven years of fishing and piloting. If anyone knew that coast, Stuart did. Back in the safety of the harbour, I picked up my box of kit and thanked Stuart for keeping me safe. He took my hand, looked directly at me, and asked me if I believed in God. I had never shared my faith with him, and he had no idea I was a Christian. It seems that the experience at the end had been quite a spiritual one for him. I smiled and told him I did believe in God and that I had been praying most of the way across the Channel. A week later, he contacted me to say he stayed up most of that night trying to find the church on Google maps. But nothing showed on any satellite picture or map. My landing point was Tardinghen Mussel Stakes, France. There is no church marked on any map there. Neither is there any building within a mile.

Although he was exhausted, Stuart was not prepared to accept that the church had just appeared because I said a few prayers. The next morning, not having slept a wink, he bought a ferry ticket to Calais, then drove along the French coast to Tardinghen. It took him several hours as there are few roads – just dirt tracks – but eventually his persistence paid off and he found a tiny chapel called St Martins. There are two days each year when the church is illuminated: 7 September 2014 just happened to be one of those days, and the lights just happened to be left on at 11.20 p.m. European Time.

The closer I get to God, the more I see him at work. He's at work all the time, everywhere; we just don't look for him. I need to keep looking up at the light. We all need to keep looking up at the light.

Resources

On this page you can find a range of organisations that will be able to help.

You can also contact the author on **info@recoverytwo.org.**

Please don't suffer in silence.

12 Step Fellowships

Alcohol
Alcoholics Anonymous
www.aa-gb.org.uk
Helpline: 0845 769 7555

Anorexia and Bulimia
Anorexics and Bulimics Anonymous
www.aba12steps.org

Cocaine
Cocaine Anonymous
www.cauk.org.uk
Helpline: 0800 612 0225

Co-Dependency
Co-Dependents Anonymous
www.coda-uk.org
Information: 07000 263645

Compulsive eating
Overeaters Anonymous
www.oagb.org.uk
Helpline: 07000 784985

Debt
Debtors Anonymous
www.debtorsanonymous.info
Information: 020 7644 5070

Depression
Depressives Anonymous
www.depressionanon.co.uk
Information line: 0870 774 4320

Drugs
Narcotics Anonymous
www.ukna.org
Helpline: 0845 3733366

Gambling
Gamblers Anonymous
www.gamblersanonymous.org.uk
National Helpline: 020 7384 3040

Sex
Sexaholics Anonymous
www.sauk.org
Helpline: 07000 725463

Sex & Love Addicts Anonymous
www.slaauk.com
Information: 07951 815087

Sex Addicts Anonymous
www.sexaa.org

Sexual Compulsives Anonymous
www.sca-recovery.org

Smoking
Nicotine Anonymous
www.nicotine-anonymous.co.uk
Information: 020 7976 0076

Christian Recovery Courses

The Recovery Course
info@recoverytwo.org
www.recoverytwo.org
therecoverycourse@googlemail.com

Celebrate Recovery
www.celebraterecovery.co.uk

Christians Against Poverty Release Course
info@capreleasegroups.org
01274 760595

Online/Browser Protection

CovernantEyes.com
www.covenanteyes.com

K9
www.k9webprotection.com